P9-BTM-929

8/16   **DATE DUE**

MASTER SWISS CHOCOLATIER
SINCE 1845

MASTER SWISS CHOCOLATIER

SINCE 1845

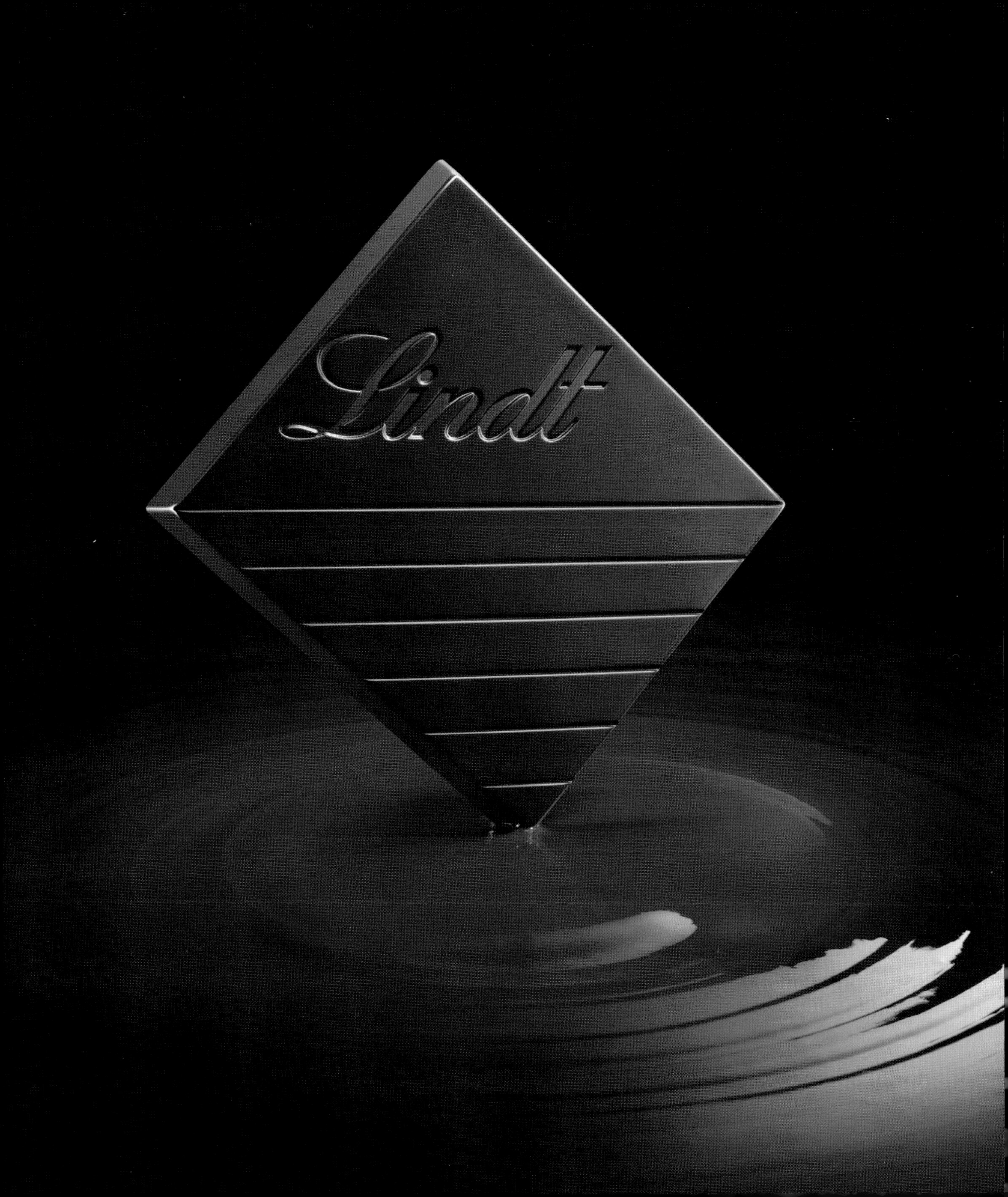
Lindt

Lindt Chocolate Passion

LINDT'S MAÎTRES CHOCOLATIERS SHARE THEIR RECIPES AND TECHNIQUES

First published in 2007 by
LINDT & SPRÜNGLI (USA)

ISBN 10 0-9798259-0-3
ISBN 13 978-1-9798259-0-3

RECIPE PHOTOGRAPHY © JIM SCHERER
FOOD STYLING BY CATRINE KELTY

PRODUCED BY SANGER COMMUNICATIONS,
5 Market Street, Portsmouth, NH
Design by Kathryn Sky-Peck
Typeset in Centaur and Englische Schreibschrift

Printed in China
10 9 8 7 6 5 4 3 2 1

DEEP APPRECIATION goes to our Maîtres Chocolatiers Hans Geller, Flora Grösslich, Jean-Pierre Larramendy, Urs Liechti, Hans Mazenauer, Hélène Mazuyer, Thomas Schnetzler, and David Vignau. Their innovative creations, following in the tradition of Rodolphe Lindt, make Lindt & Sprüngli the renowned chocolate manufacturer that it is today.

Ann Czaja, Maître Chocolatier, Lindt & Sprüngli USA, was indispensable in the preparation and proofing of this manuscript. The magnificent recipes in this volume were developed by her and her fellow Maîtres Chocolatiers around the globe, and her ability to coordinate this collaboration is deeply appreciated.

Christine Bullen, Vice President of Retail, Laura Howson, Design Consultant, and Sheryl Frazier, Promotions Manager, oversaw this project for Lindt & Sprüngli (USA) Inc. Without their guidance and expertise, this book would not have been possible.

Grateful acknowledgement goes to Thomas Linemayr, President of Lindt & Sprüngli (USA) Inc., for his support and encouragement.

ACKNOWLEDGEMENTS

CONTENTS

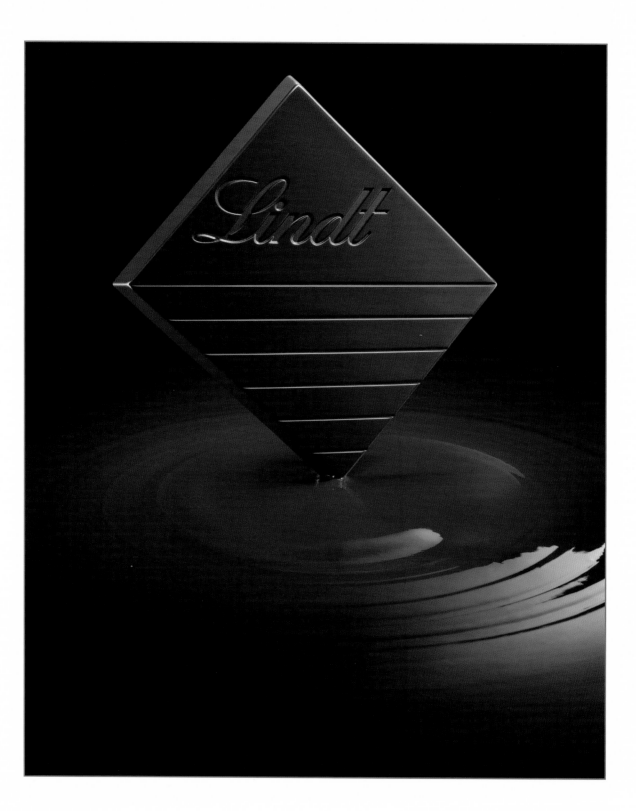

THE ANCIENT MAYA, who most experts agree were the first to discover cacao, believed that cocoa was a gift from the gods. Anyone who has tasted Lindt's little bit of heaven, the Lindor® truffle, might very well agree. The Lindor truffle is loved around the world for its exquisite chocolate taste and creamy, silky texture. However, the truffle is just one of the many delicious creations my fellow Maîtres Chocolatiers and I have been developing for Lindt & Sprüngli, in a tradition of excellence that dates back to 1845. In this book you'll discover how truly versatile chocolate can be.

Everyone associates chocolate with love, and indeed, this book is a labor of love for all of us. Here, in *Lindt Chocolate Passion*, Lindt's Maîtres Chocolatiers (French for "Master Chocolatiers") share with you for the first time the personal recipes and techniques we use at home when cooking and entertaining for family and friends. Though we live and work on three continents, we all share one thing in common: an absolute passion for Lindt® chocolate. We use only the finest and purest ingredients of unequaled quality, flavor, and appearance in our chocolate, and we know you are going to love tasting the wonderful recipes you are about to create!

When you think about Switzerland, you probably think: Chocolate! Many of the pioneers of the chocolate industry were Swiss, and Lindt & Sprüngli is no exception. Rodolphe Lindt was a Maître Chocolatier in Bern, Switzerland, in the mid-nineteenth century, and he was passionate about his profession. Before Lindt developed his unique production process, chocolate did not have the velvety-smooth, melt-in-your-mouth quality that it has today. His dedication and commitment to excellence drove Lindt to revolutionize the industry and ignite an obsession for chocolate that has spread to all parts of the globe. Lindt's passion, combined with the entrepreneurial spirit of Johann Rudolf Sprüngli-Schifferli, enabled what was once an aristocratic luxury to be savored nearly anywhere on this planet.

FOREWORD

Today we continue in the tradition of our founders and strive to bring our customers the finest premium chocolate. Exceptional artisans who have spent years learning the art, science, history, and business of chocolate, our Maîtres Chocolatiers still oversee every aspect of Lindt's chocolate production, just as Rodolphe Lindt did, from selecting only the finest cacao beans and ingredients from around the world to creating our exciting new recipes and products. I consider it a great honor to have been chosen as Lindt's Maître Chocolatier for the United States, and a real joy to help bring this book to you.

When Lindt USA decided to create this special book, it was only natural that we would reach out to our Maîtres Chocolatiers around the world. My colleagues and I studied the art of chocolate as apprentices in Europe and learned from masters of the craft. It sounds like a dream job, right? I certainly think so! You can read more about our Maîtres Chocolatiers and our training on page 11.

At Lindt, we pursue chocolate excellence every day. By sharing our favorite recipes and professional tips, we hope that you will ultimately discover the chocolatier in you.

—Ann Czaja

PROBABLY EVERY CHOCOLATE LOVER marvels at its magical qualities. How on earth did mere mortals come upon something so delectable? Swedish botanist Carl von Linné (Linnaeus) rightly named the cacao tree's genus *theobroma*, from the Greek for "food of the gods." No description could be more appropriate. But how did this bitter, unpromising bean make the mysterious leap to the chocolate we love today?

Not even historians can agree on the actual genesis of chocolate. We know that in the first millennium B.C., the cacao's large, brightly colored, football-shaped pods probably beckoned to the Mesoamericans of the time—the Olmec and Maya. Although the raw, almond-sized cacao seed has a bitter taste, the pod's inner soft pulp has a sweet, lemony flavor and is thirst quenching. It is only natural that someone eventually looked past the gooey fruit to investigate the seed inside. Given the approach to most pre-Columbian cooking in Mesoamerica, the seeds would have been gathered, laid out in the sun to dry, and then ground on stone slabs, using the same techniques applied to other everyday foods such as corn, chilies, and pumpkin seeds.

Grinding the sun-dried cacao seeds would have also released their natural oils, and the process would have produced a fragrant paste that, once discovered, would have become an irresistible ingredient of drinks and other foods. These earliest Mesoamericans accomplished the feat of recognizing the importance of the cacao tree and domesticating it for their use. Generations of experimentation led to knowledge of a range of culinary possibilities for the cacao paste. Over the centuries to follow, the Maya became more sophisticated in their methods of fermenting, roasting, and grinding the cacao seeds. Sometimes mixed with corn meal, cacao was a significant source of nutrition and energy, and became such an important part of the Mayan diet and culture that Maya believed cacao was a gift from the gods. Cacao paste was popularly mixed with chili peppers to make a foamy, spicy chocolate drink called *xocoatl* (pronounced like "sho-cot-al"),

meaning "bitter water." This is most likely the origin of our word "chocolate."

When the Aztecs conquered large portions of Mexico in the 14th century, they were quick to assimilate cacao into their culture. As they expanded their territory, they began to demand tributes of cacao seeds from conquered tribes. Eventually the Aztecs valued the seeds so highly they used them as a form of currency. A basket of 400 cacao beans was known as one zontli and 8,000 beans equaled one xiquipilli. In just a few hundred years, cacao had become a symbol of divine beneficence and health, as well as wealth and power in Mesoamerica.

Above: An offering of chocolate in this painting on a Late Classic Maya vase. Below: An Aztec statue of a man holding a cacao pod.

On Christopher Columbus's fourth voyage to America in 1502, he encountered a group of native Americans off the coast of Honduras who seemed to be unusually protective of a large horde of "nuts" they carried in their canoe. Columbus was thus the first European to come in contact with the cacao bean but, unfamiliar with the native language, he had no idea what the precious cargo was. Its value remained a mystery until Hernando Cortés invaded Mexico.

By the time the Spanish arrived on the Mexican coast in the 1520s, cacao was probably the most valuable traded item on the mainland. The value of cacao was not lost on Cortés when he conquered the Aztecs in the 16th century. When Cortés observed the emperor Montezuma drinking the frothed cacao with a high degree of ceremony, Cortés recognized cacao as an exalted food, and that it was also often included along with gold and gems in ceremonial offerings. He took a literal view of it as currency, for he wasn't as keen about chocolate's bitter flavor. He immediately established in the name of Spain a cacao plantation where, henceforth, "money" would be cultivated. On his return to Europe in 1528, Cortés embarked with the first cacao beans and a recipe to produce xocoatl for King Charles V of Spain. It was the Spanish who first added sugar to cacao; sugar was unknown in pre-Hispanic Mexico, and was itself carried back to Spain from the sugar cane trade in the Spanish territories of the Caribbean. Although the recipe for xocoatl was thus altered for sweetness for its European debut, one thing

about it didn't change: it was still very much reserved for royalty and those of high social standing.

When the Spanish princess Anna of Austria married Louis XIII in 1615, chocolate was introduced to French nobility. From France, the beverage traveled to England where the first chocolate shop was opened in 1657, and as early as 1674 chocolate was being baked, "Spanish style," in cakes and rolls.

The first record of established cocoa plantations is a royal decree dated November 1, 1677, granted to Brazil, in the state of Para. Meanwhile, back in Europe, chocolate made its way from the west to the east, through Brussels, where Heinrich Escher, mayor of Zurich, first tasted the drink and brought his accounts of it back home. Frederick I of Prussia imposed a tax on chocolate in 1704, making anyone who wanted to indulge in it pay two thalers.

In 1711, when Emperor Charles VI transferred his court from Madrid to Vienna, chocolate made its way to Italy. As early as 1720, the coffee houses of Florence and Venice gained international reputations for offering chocolate. Italian chocolatiers, well-versed in the art of making chocolate, were consequently welcome visitors in France, Germany, and Switzerland. In 1755, chocolate's travels came full circle when it was reintroduced to America by way of the colonists.

But Switzerland became the true epicenter in the modern history of chocolate. The Swiss pioneered most of the major advances in the taste and manufacture of chocolate in the nineteenth century. The first Swiss chocolate factory was set up in 1819, in a former mill near Vevey. The founder, François-Louis Cailler, had learned the secrets of the chocolate-making trade in Italy. Daniel Peter made the world's first milk chocolate, also in Vevey, in 1875. He added condensed milk invented by his friend and neighbor Henri Nestlé in 1867. Another famous Swiss chocolatier to emerge was Jean Tobler, who began selling his famous triangular chocolate Toblerone in 1899.

Most of these advances in chocolate production were made possible in 1828, when Dutchman Hendrick Van Houten invented the cocoa press, which further helped reduce the price of cocoa and improve the quality of the beverage by squeezing out part of the cocoa butter (fat that naturally occurs in cacao beans), and allowed the cocoa to be ground more finely. From then on, drinking chocolate had more of the smooth consistency and pleasing flavor it has today. Today, this process is known as "dutching." The final product, Dutch chocolate, has a dark

color and mild taste. In 1847, Fry's chocolate factory in Bristol, England molded the first chocolate bar that, although somewhat crumbly, was suitable for general consumption.

However, in spite of chocolate's seemingly rapid evolution, it was about to take a giant leap forward when Lindt & Sprüngli entered the world of chocolate manufacturing, and forever changed what we think of as chocolate.

LINDT'S PLACE IN CHOCOLATE HISTORY

The story of Lindt & Sprüngli began on the shores of Switzerland's Lake Zurich in 1845 when confectioners David Sprüngli and his son Rudolf Sprüngli-Ammann opened their first small chocolate factory. David and Rudolf were passionate confectioners and loved experimenting with new chocolate recipes. They soon earned a reputation as Zurich's most talented chocolatiers and Sprüngli chocolate became the favorite of Zurich's high society and the first popular confectionery in the German-speaking part of Switzerland. To meet the demand for their chocolate, Sprüngli & Son opened a larger factory in 1859 that included an elegant new café where Zurich's fashionable families could come to sip hot chocolate and sample Sprüngli's many chocolate luxuries. It soon became hugely popular and a tremendous success. By 1870, it was necessary to build a third, even larger Sprüngli factory to keep up with demand.

Meanwhile in Bern, a young Swiss entrepreneur named Rodolphe Lindt was about to revolutionize the world of chocolate. To the amusement of the burghers of Bern, Rodolphe announced he intended to manufacture chocolate. At that time, the commercially available chocolate was either drinking chocolate or a rather crumbly paste that was sometimes formed into a crude bar. It had a distinctly gritty and grainy texture, a quality that was intrinsic to the food itself—not at all the refined product that we know and love today.

In 1879, the 24-year-old Rodolphe Lindt bought two fire damaged factories and a second-hand cacao bean roasting machine. And then—no one knows whether by accident or by design—Rodolphe left the chocolate machine on for an unprecedented three days. The chocolate it produced was miraculous. Dark, silky smooth with a glorious sheen, it melted on the tongue (chocolate at that time had to be chewed) and released a wealth of delicious flavors. Young Rodolphe christened his new creation *chocolat fondant* ("melting chocolate") and chocolate as we know it was born.

That same year, Lindt set about perfecting his technique for manufacturing his *chocolat fondant*, and eventually devised an apparatus called a "conche" (after the Spanish word for shell, *concha*) that could process the cocoa paste into a chocolate of unprecedented smoothness, delicate flavor, and that had a silky way of melting. Lindt's process of "conching" involved rolling the cocoa paste for many hours—which produced its own internal warming—with the addition of cocoa butter to achieve the creamy quality for which Lindt's "melting chocolate" became renowned and contributed significantly to the worldwide reputation of Swiss chocolate. Lindt's new incarnation of chocolate was a sensation. No one had ever tasted anything like it before. It became the new standard against which all chocolate was held.

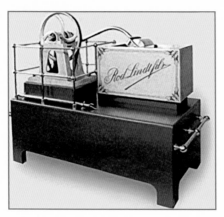

Rodolphe Lindt's revolutionary invention: the "conche."

For the next 20 years, Lindt's competitors tried desperately to learn his conching technique and secret recipe. Finally, in 1899, the Sprüngli Chocolate Company paid Rodolphe Lindt 675,000 francs in an advance for his trade secrets, and would pay almost one million more francs for the conching machines and to retain him as partner in the company. It was an incredible offer, the equivalent of 100 million dollars today. We can thank Johann Rudolf Sprüngli-Schifferli, who had taken over the Sprüngli factory from his father, for this daring and bold move. It created one of the most famous manufacturers of Swiss chocolate and, most importantly, one of the creamiest and tastiest premium chocolates in the world.

It seemed as if industrial advances and transportation improvements conspired to place Rudolf Sprüngli and Rodolphe Lindt at the zenith of chocolate manufacturing in spite of their sometimes fractious partnership. Outside of the company, the world was going through tremendous change as well, including world-wide war. Rather than give up in the face of shortage, the innovative spirit of Lindt & Sprüngli met the hardship of war and turned out new products to deal with raw material shortages while keeping production levels stable and quality high. The company's tradition has always been about paying attention to current social trends and investing in technological improvements accordingly, in order to meet future trends, and to persevere in its commitment to quality and innovation, while making the most number of people happy—from its employees to its customers all over the globe.

LINDT & SPRÜNGLI TODAY

Today, Chocoladefabriken Lindt & Sprüngli AG is an iconic world leader and pioneer in the premium chocolate market, known for its innovation and creativity. A company that embraces and celebrates its unique Swiss heritage and rich tradition for chocolate making, Lindt & Sprüngli has, over the past century, experienced meteoric growth, with manufacturing sites in Switzerland, Germany, France, Italy, the U.S.A., and Austria. Lindt has sales and distribution companies in England, Poland, Spain, Canada, Australia, Mexico, and Sweden, and sales offices in Hong Kong and Dubai. As a member of the World Cocoa Foundation (WCF), Lindt & Sprüngli is dedicated to sustainable cocoa farming practices and purchases the world's finest grade cacao beans to ensure pure, delicious chocolate flavors.

For over 160 years, recipes have been created, collected, refined, proved, and old recipes have been mixed with new ones to create the incomparable Lindt chocolates. Lindt is constantly recreating and refining its production processes, and has done so continuously over its long history. The combination of innovation and ingenuity has contributed significantly to Lindt's longevity and measurable success.

Lindt cuts no corners in its pursuit of creating the best quality chocolate available in order to provide the ultimate chocolate experience and indulgence.

CREATING PREMIUM CHOCOLATE IS AN ART that requires great skill, dedication and passion, and the Maîtres Chocolatiers of Lindt are masters of this craft. Every production site of the Lindt & Sprüngli Group has its own Maître Chocolatier team further refining and enhancing Lindt's basic, dark, white, and milk chocolate, as well as the Lindor and Excellence™ range of recipes into innovative products.

We develop and refine our unique secret recipes with absolute devotion. Attention is lavished on Lindt chocolate, starting with the selection of the finest raw materials and highest-quality ingredients, and culminating in the final exquisite creations. With unfailing commitment to detail, we decorate chocolates with elegance, and wrap and present them as preciously as jewels.

The trademark *Lindt*® is the guarantee for premium chocolate of distinct smoothness, characteristic taste, and innovative flair. Every single piece is created by our unmatched passion for high-quality chocolate. It's a tradition the Lindt Maîtres Chocolatiers have carried on since 1845.

Innovative flair—and the creativity and the passion behind it—are hallmarks of Lindt's Maîtres Chocolatiers. Much more than iconic, we are honored to be considered the heart and soul of Lindt. We are involved in all facets of chocolate production. We select the beans, supervise the roasting process, and develop the secret recipes that make Lindt chocolate so extraordinary.

We craft new combinations of the world's finest and rarest cocoa beans and take years to research, develop, test, and perfect the most delectable chocolate bars and seasonal treats. Our skill and expertise are responsible for the premium products that Lindt proudly offers our discriminating customers.

With Lindt you experience the ultimate chocolate delight.

THE LINDT MAÎTRES CHOCOLATIERS

As Lindt Maîtres Chocolatiers, we create a wide range of chocolates, but the one that is probably most iconic is the classic Lindor truffle. Inspired by Lindt's secret recipe, our masterpiece truffle is a delicious Lindt chocolate shell enrobing an irresistibly smooth filling that melts in the mouth—and has melted the hearts of all who have tried it.

Biting into this chocolate, you recapture the enchantment that must have been the first taste of Rodolphe Lindt's history-making chocolate fondant. The sensation is that luxurious, silky, and pure, and true to the Lindt tradition.

Excellence is a unique chocolate that reveals all the strength and richness of cacao beans. To fully appreciate its flavor and texture, we recommend that you progressively develop your palate through our range of high cocoa content chocolate bars, starting with Excellence 70% cocoa, then 85%, and finally 99% cocoa. To best experience Excellence, taste a small piece and let it melt in your mouth.

Excellence is the chocolate that you will find most often specified for the recipes in this book. This revolutionary innovation in chocolate captures the true depth and range of cocoa, from white chocolate, to milk chocolate, to dark chocolate.

If a single bar could capture the passion of the Maîtres Chocolatiers, it would be Excellence. This is chocolate at its absolute finest.

Featured on these two pages:
Facing page: Lindt Excellence 99% Cocoa; Top: Lindt Excellence Extra Creamy Milk Chocolate; below: Excellence White Coconut.

Although Lindor and Excellence are the iconic Lindt chocolates, the Maîtres Chocolatiers are constantly creating and developing new confections. Creating boxes of pralines is the most challenging, and can take up to two and a half years to develop. Each chocolate has to be different, but the combination of design and taste must also be perfectly balanced.

The Petits Desserts™ are another example of the innovation and inspiration that drive our creations. Each Petit Dessert marries Lindt's legendary art of chocolate making with a classic dessert recipe like Meringue, Crème Brûlée, Lemon Tart, Tiramisu, Chocolate Log, Brownie, or Macaroon.

 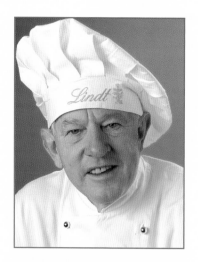 

ALL OF LINDT'S MAÎTRES CHOCOLATIERS are European-trained, in rigorous yet practical programs that take several years to complete. In Switzerland, for example, the traditional training involves an apprenticeship. The aspiring Maîtres Chocolatiers study pastry and chocolate arts by attending school one day a week and working in a patisserie/confiserie (pastry/confectionery shop) the remaining four days, under the watchful eye of highly-skilled teachers with years of hands-on experience. Following the completion of the three-year training, the student takes a final practical exam in addition to the written and oral exams. Upon successful completion of the requirements the student is awarded certification by Switzerland.

An additional two-year program is required to get a master's degree, which is pursued by individuals who aspire to own a business, rise to the rank of executive pastry chef, or participate in international culinary competitions. Others complete the master's credentials in order to teach.

To bring you the recipes in this book, Lindt invited our Maîtres Chocolatiers from around the globe to share some of their favorite creations. You'll find that each recipe will be credited with the name of the Maître Chocolatier who created it, and in the true spirit of Lindt's global family of Maîtres Chocolatiers, many of these recipes are collaborations.

ANN CZAJA

Swiss-trained American Maître Chocolatier Ann Czaja worked for Lindt & Sprüngli in Switzerland before returning to the U.S.A. While living and working in Zürich for nearly 14 years, Ann had the opportunity to study pastry and chocolate from the world's foremost authorities. It was a very intense but rewarding experience. Her advice to anyone interested in entering the profession is to treat the chocolate with respect, because it can be extremely temperamental.

One of the things that Ann is most passionate about is the rich cultural history of chocolate. She thinks it is an amazing natural product and enjoys talking about it almost as much as working with it.

HANS GELLER

Hans Geller is a retired Swiss Maître Chocolatier. He ran the product development team for Lindt & Sprüngli in Kilchberg, Switzerland for many years. His advice

Facing page: the Lindt Maîtres Chocolatiers:

Top row: Ann Czaja, Hans Geller, Hans Mazenauer
Middle row: Flora Grösslich, Urs Liechti, Jean-Pierre Larramendy
Bottom row: David Vignau, Hélène Mazuyer, Thomas Schnetzler

to anyone aspiring to enter the profession is to pursue good basic training and keep learning—always be on the lookout for new trends and interesting flavor combinations.

FLORA GRÖSSLICH

Flora is an Austrian Maître Chocolatier and works in product development for Lindt & Sprüngli, Austria. Flora cultivated a taste for fine Swiss chocolate while working there as a pastry chef. She considers chocolate the ultimate taste experience and enjoys combining it with interesting raw ingredients. "The most fulfilling aspect of my job," says Flora, "is creating chocolates that will put a smile on the face of even the grumpiest person. The look in the eyes of a person enjoying chocolate-inspired delight is indescribable." Flora believes that technique and knowledge of food science can be learned, but the passion for the work must be present before you begin.

JEAN-PIERRE LARRAMENDY

Jean-Pierre Larramendy, Maître Chocolatier at Lindt & Sprüngli in France, and a self-proclaimed chocolate gourmand, is most fascinated with the chocolate manufacturing process. Following new technologies involved in chocolate manufacture and refining recipes helps him continuously acquire new skills, which he finds very gratifying. But even more gratifying for Jean-Pierre is seeing a new product get put into production and, finally, the pleasure people experience when they taste a square of chocolate—seeing the joy in their eyes, and hearing them exclaim, "This is delicious!" In order to be a good Maître Chocolatier, Jean-Pierre believes one must be curious, always researching new technologies, and have a thirst for learning; to be very self-disciplined and take a lot of pleasure in one's work. He gets a great deal of pleasure from experimenting with new tastes and different textures.

URS LIECHTI

Urs Liechti is a Swiss Maître Chocolatier who currently runs the product development team in Kilchberg, Switzerland. He finds his job exciting and enjoys the creativity of working with pure and high quality chocolate. Urs ran his own confectionery for 10 years before coming to Lindt and often says that he is living his dream. Seeing the test products going from his lab to the factory and finally on the shelves in stores is for Urs absolutely amazing.

Urs recommends that anyone wanting to enter the profession should have good ideas and creativity involving recipe development and flavor combinations.

As for Urs, he never tires of chocolate and even has a piece on his days off. "I eat between 100 and 150 grams of chocolate a day," says Urs. "I'm the luckiest guy in the world."

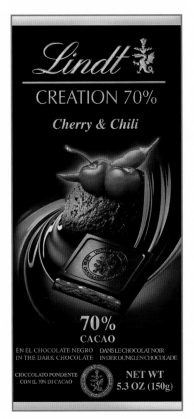

HANS MAZENAUER

Hans Mazenauer is a retired Swiss Maître Chocolatier who finished his long career working with Lindt & Sprüngli USA. Part of his duties included educating the company's retail staff members about chocolate. In his 50-year career he witnessed the transition from hand-making pralines and chocolate to using machinery that revolutionized the business, and he feels fortunate to have been a part of ensuring that the quality always remained. One of his proudest achievements was being named in Who's Who of Professionals for the year 2000. Having traveled the globe extensively, Hans now calls Florida home.

Hans's advice to would-be Maître Chocolatiers: have a passion for chocolate and an interest to learn all aspects of the job, from the fresh bean to the finished product.

HÉLÈNE MAZUYER

French Maître Chocolatier and confectioner Hélène Mazuyer worked in small, artisan confectioneries before she began at Lindt, where she realized her dream to work for a large-scale chocolatier, sharing her experience and specialized knowledge with a wider audience. She is most interested in the diverse ways in which chocolate can be worked—carved, shaped, or molded—while playing with color to add a splash of fantasy. Hélène enjoys experimenting with chocolate to discover the new flavor combinations that Lindt chocolate lovers eagerly anticipate. For Hélène, chocolate is not just a craving; it's a daily exercise, to keep her palate in shape and sensitize it to different aromas and textures. She feels that chocolate should be a source of wonder that recaptures the sweetness of childhood and believes that, much in the way a jeweler creates a gemstone out of a rock, chocolate-making should always be a creative endeavor. Her fondest wish is to ensure that the magic of chocolate continues to create a spark of delight in everyone's eyes. Hélène says that the key to being a Maître Chocolatier is above all being passionate and having a creative, artistic side. "It's best to have golden fingertips, for the profession is one of finesse, agility, and patience."

THOMAS SCHNETZLER

Thomas Schnetzler is a Swiss Maître Chocolatier who lives in Australia. He has been in the country for nearly 10 years and enjoys his job with Lindt & Sprüngli, Australia. He loves the versatility of chocolate. You can bake it, carve it, and even experiment with it, spending many hours creating something beautiful. Growing up in Switzerland, Thomas was fascinated with the beautiful Easter bunnies displayed in local chocolate shops. His biggest challenge is getting all of the chefs in Australia to temper their chocolate. His instructions on tempering are featured in this book.

Thomas believes that in order to be a good Maître Chocolatier, in addition to having a good eye and patience, you must try what you are making.

DAVID VIGNAU

French Maître Chocolatier David Vignau had extensive experience as a pastry chef and confectioner before starting at Lindt in France 11 years ago. If you asked David Vignau what he loves most, he'd say, "Chocolate!" Art, however, is his true passion; for he likes to invent, and create, to spend time thinking about new trends, tastes, and unusual textures. His goal is to always surprise consumers with his creativity. David was drawn to the chocolate industry because it allows him to satisfy his passion for chocolate-making through its various technologies and processes, that is, converting cacao beans into a chocolate. To be a successful Maître Chocolatier, David feels it's not enough to be fond of chocolate and be creative; one must be passionate, persevering, a perfectionist, and accept that it takes time, patience, and study. Furthermore, David believes that team spirit is absolutely necessary to conceive, create, make, and sell Lindt's exceptional final product.

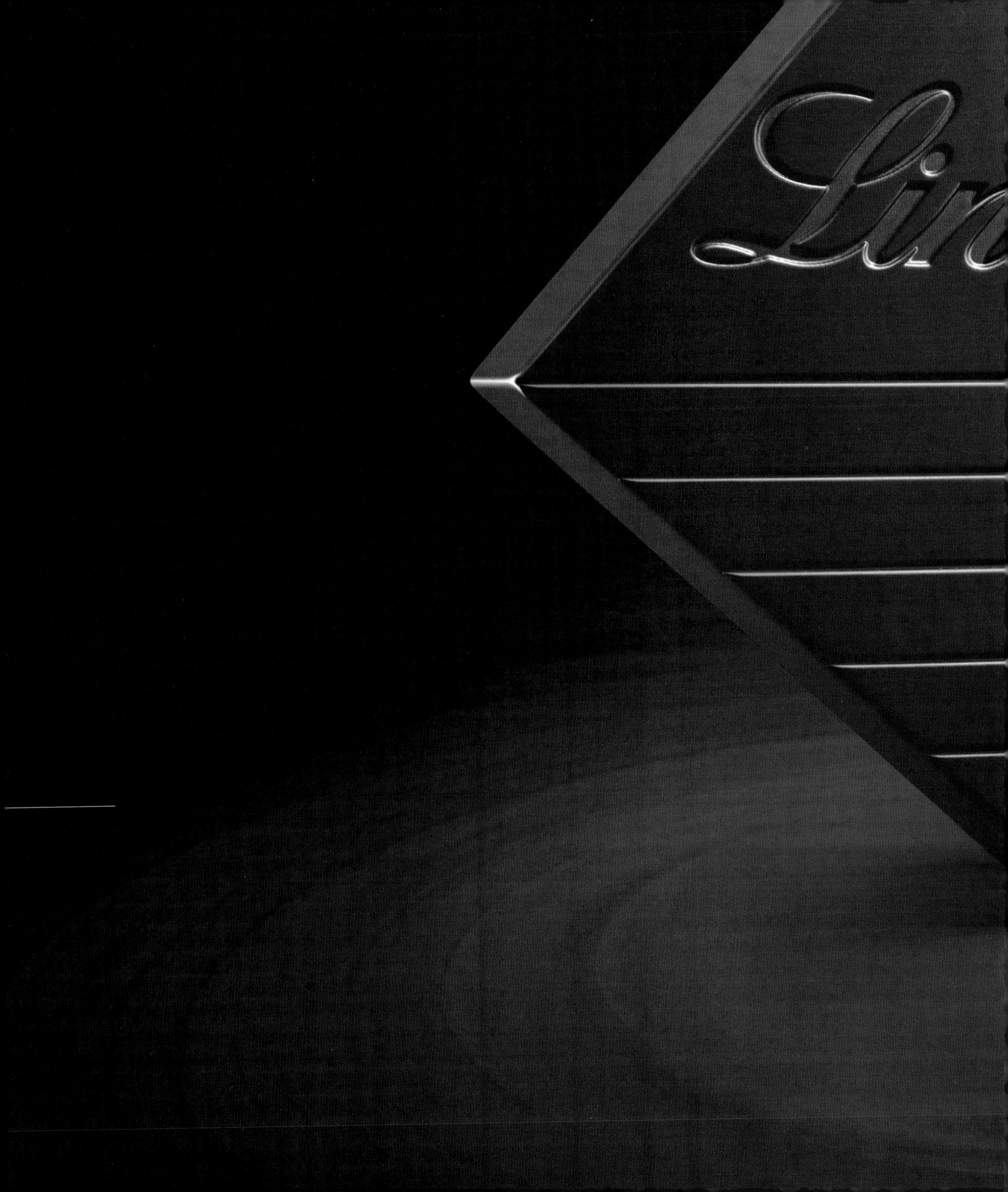

Chocolate Basics

CHOCOLATE. COULD ANY ONE ingredient be more glorious? Yet the cacao bean—the heart of the sweetest delicacy in the world—is bitter. In this chapter you'll get an overview of how the bitter cacao bean becomes transformed into chocolate. You'll also learn about the different forms chocolate can take, from cocoa powder, to unsweetened chocolate, dark chocolate, milk chocolate, and white chocolate.

When you're cooking with chocolate, using a premium product will result in a creation of the highest quality and most delicious taste, and to that end you can rely on Lindt chocolate. Each recipe presented in this book specifies the type of Lindt chocolate to use, and this chapter will provide you an overview of the different qualities of each type.

The following is a general introduction to how cacao is processed into chocolate, and an review of the distinctions among the varieties of chocolate that are available today, from bittersweet to milk to white. Due to the premium nature of Lindt's chocolate and processes, Lindt has many additional proprietary and special secret recipes that ensure the high quality of our chocolate, which go beyond this general introduction. We present you here with a quick tour through the world of chocolate production in an effort to give you a better sense of this wonderful ingredient you'll be working with.

CHOCOLATE PRODUCTION

The cacao tree can flourish only in the hottest regions of the world, between 20° north and south of the equator, making South America and Africa the optimal cultivation regions. There are three main classifications of cacao beans: criollo, forastero, and trinitario. Criollo is the high-quality bean revered by the Maya and it grows in central and northern South America, mainly in its native Ecuador and

The cacao pods, just before harvest.

Venezuela. It is classified as a flavor bean and accounts for approximately five percent of the world cacao bean harvest.

The pure variety of the criollo bean is of finer quality than that of the forastero variety, which is a much hardier, higher-yielding plant that produces about 90 percent of the world harvest. The forastero family, with its many hybrids and varieties, originated in the Amazon River basin and today is grown mainly in West Africa, as well as in Brazil. Most forastero beans are classified as bulk beans and used in blends; one exception is Arriba, from Ecuador, which is classified as a flavor bean.

Trinitario, a flavor bean, is a hybrid of criollo and forastero, and it originated in Trinidad. Accounting for approximately five percent of the world harvest, trinitario often combines the best traits of it parents. It exhibits a greater resistance to disease than criollo, but often has a fine, aromatic flavor.

There are two annual harvests, generally in March and October, which are still done by hand. Each cacao tree can produce between 20 and 50 pods containing between 25 and 50 seeds each. Once the pods are removed from the tree, they are cut open and the seeds and pulp are removed and allowed to ferment four to seven days. Fermentation is an important process that reduces the natural bitter flavor and astringency of the beans. New flavors start to develop that will become the familiar cocoa aroma during the drying and roasting phases. After fermentation, the beans are dried for one to two weeks. The drying process reduces the water naturally contained in the bean, and its color starts to deepen.

After arriving in Switzerland, the imported raw cacao is subject to a strict quality control. If the result of the quality test is satisfactory, the raw cacao is first stored before undergoing further processing. Before the real processing begins, the raw cacao is thoroughly cleaned by passing through sieves and by brushing. Finally, the last vestiges of any natural impurities, and even the finest dust, are extracted by powerful vacuum equipment.

Similar to coffee, cacao beans are dried and roasted before being hulled. The purpose of the roasting process, in furnaces set between 250°F (120°C) and 300°F

(150°C), is primarily to develop the aroma. The roasted beans are then cracked and winnowed to remove the nib of the cacao bean from its shell.

Before the nibs go through a finer grinding process, they are weighed and blended according to special recipes. The secret of every chocolate factory lies in the special mixing ratios it has developed for different types of cocoa.

Now the crushed cacao beans are ready for grinding. Still fairly coarse, the beans are pre-ground by special milling equipment and then fed onto rollers where they are further ground into a fine paste. The heat generated by the resulting pressure and friction causes the cocoa butter (approximately 50 percent of the bean) to melt, producing a thick, liquid mixture. This is dark brown in color with a characteristic, strong odor. During cooling it gradually sets: this is the cocoa paste, also known as cocoa liquor.

At this point the production process divides into two paths: One part of the cocoa liquor is taken to large presses that extract the cocoa butter. The other part passes through various blending and refining processes during which some of the cocoa butter is added to it, and here the two paths rejoin. The cocoa butter has important functions. It not only forms part of every recipe, but it also later gives the chocolate its fine structure, beautiful luster, and delicate, attractive glaze.

What about that part of the cocoa paste on the first path, the one not rejoined with cocoa butter? After the cocoa butter has left the press, the pasty compressed cocoa that remains still comprises between 10 and 20 percent fat, depending on the intensity of compression. These compressed cocoa "cakes" are crushed again, ground to powder, and finely sifted in several stages until transformed into a dark, strongly aromatic powder, namely cocoa powder.

Once the cocoa is processed, the chocolate manufacture can begin with combining the three to four basic ingredients for making chocolate: cocoa liquor, cocoa butter, sugar, and milk. By blending them in accordance with specific recipes, three types of chocolate are obtained that form the basis of every product assortment, namely:

- Dark chocolate: cocoa liquor + cocoa butter + sugar
- Milk chocolate: cocoa liquor + cocoa butter + sugar + milk
- White chocolate: cocoa butter + sugar + milk

Once blended, the mixture gets milled by steel rollers that reduce tiny particles of cocoa and sugar to microscopic sizes. Then the chocolate undergoes the conching process. As a result, the chocolate is now velvety smooth. An additional benefit of the conching process is aeration. Any remaining bitterness in the cocoa liquor evaporates. Before the forming or molding process, the chocolate must be tempered: heated, cooled, and reheated to achieve the perfect finish and set. Tempering gives the set chocolate a soft luster, matte sheen, and rounded flavor. Finally, the chocolate is formed into bars or molded into other products, wrapped, and packed for distribution.

Chocolate varieties are classified according to cocoa percentage, or how much unsweetened cocoa liquor they contain.

COCOA POWDER

Ground press cake containing only 10 to 20 percent cocoa butter, cocoa powder is excellent for preparing delicious drinks such as traditional hot cocoa. It's also frequently called for in baking, and is used as a dusting for cakes and a garnish for truffles and mousse.

UNSWEETENED CHOCOLATE

100 percent cocoa: As the name implies, this has no added sugar. Although unsweetened chocolate has an intense flavor, it also may have a lower cocoa butter content and a less smooth texture than other chocolates, so save it strictly for recipes where it will be combined with other ingredients.

Although not strictly an unsweetened bar, Lindt's Excellence 99% Cocoa is a unique chocolate that reveals all the strength and richness of cacao beans, and can be used in recipes calling for unsweetened chocolate.

COUVERTURE

High-quality milk, white, or dark chocolate for eating or cooking, couverture must contain a minimum of 31 percent cocoa butter.

DARK CHOCOLATE

Including bittersweet, semisweet, and extra dark, these chocolates have a cocoa liquor content of 35 percent or higher. Products labeled "semisweet" are more prevalent in the United States than Europe; semisweet chocolate's cocoa content tends to range between 52 to 65 percent and may have more sugar than those labeled bittersweet, but many chefs use bittersweet and semisweet interchangeably. Semisweet makes a great chocolate for dipping and is good to start out working with because the lower cocoa butter content makes it a little easier to work with. Those chocolates listed at 75 percent cocoa liquor are referred to as extra dark, extra bitter, or high cocoa content dark chocolate, and chocolate that is between 65 and 75 percent cocoa can be considered bittersweet. Although bittersweets are a standard favorite for many chefs, their higher cocoa content can make working with them trickier—be sure to read the sections on tempering and ganache if you work with a high cocoa content chocolate. You'll have to manage your temperatures carefully.

Our recommendations for the recipes in this book are Lindt's Swiss Bittersweet—a classic bar—as well as Lindt's Excellence 85% Cocoa (still with a very intense cocoa flavor), and Excellence 70% Cocoa.

The connoisseur in you will appreciate the Excellence Ecuador 75% Cocoa, with the full-bodied aroma of the exquisite Arriba cocoa, which grows in the tropical coastal areas of the Ecuadorian lowlands. This is an aromatic

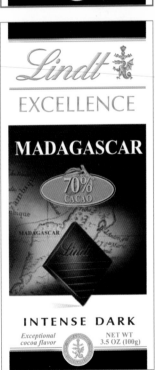

chocolate offering an intense note of cocoa. Similar to this bar is Lindt Excellence Madagascar 70% Cocoa. The exotic taste of the Sambirano cocoa, grown in the northwestern part of the island of Madagascar, imbues this prestigious chocolate with a soft and harmonious character, enriched with a hint of vanilla.

MILK CHOCOLATE

Cocoa liquor combined with cocoa butter, sugar, and milk, this chocolate is just about every kid's favorite. The minimum cocoa liquor content as mandated by the U.S. government is 10 percent by weight, although Lindt's milk chocolate contains more.

Lindt's Excellence Extra Creamy is exceptionally smooth and creamy, with the authentic taste of milk chocolate. The Swiss Classic Bars are created with the original Swiss chocolate recipe developed with passion and dedication by Lindt Maître Chocolatiers.

WHITE CHOCOLATE

Since white chocolate does not contain cocoa solids, it is technically not a chocolate. White chocolate is an ivory-colored, rich and creamy confection of cocoa butter, sugar, and milk. For the recipes that call for white chocolate, use Lindt's Swiss Classic White Chocolate.

White chocolate is delicate and scorches easily, so it should always be melted over very low heat. Because it does not contain cocoa liquor, it sets up softer than dark chocolate. White chocolate can be used for decoration of milk or dark chocolate confections or in any way the chocolates might be used.

STORING CHOCOLATE

Due to chocolate's delicate and fragile nature, it is heat sensitive. To preserve the quality of premium chocolate, it should be stored in a cool, dry place, at temperatures between 60°F (16°C) and 68°F (20°C). Humidity should be around 50 percent. If the chocolate has been opened, make sure that it is wrapped in foil and placed in an airtight bag.

If these conditions are not possible to achieve in your home, then the chocolate may be stored in the refrigerator. It is very important to make sure that it is wrapped and sealed in an airtight bag. If not, chocolate will absorb other odors from the refrigerator. When you are ready to use the chocolate, leave it in the airtight bag and allow it to come to room temperature slowly. This step will help prevent condensation on the surface of the chocolate. While refrigerating chocolate can extend its shelf life by 25 percent, it is not without risk. Improperly done, refrigeration can cause fat and sugar bloom. Never re-refrigerate chocolate once it has reached room temperature.

Chocolate may also be frozen, but this process is not recommended for filled products such as Lindor truffles. While freezing chocolate can increase its shelf life up to 50 percent, it is more complicated than refrigeration and isn't recommended. If you feel you must freeze it for future use, the chocolate should be well wrapped and place in an airtight freezer bag. When you're ready to use it, remove the chocolate from the freezer and, leaving it packed in its airtight bag, put it in the refrigerator to thaw for about six hours. Once it is thawed, proceed as described above, letting it slowly come to room temperature before you remove it from the bag. Never re-freeze chocolate once it has thawed.

YOU DON'T NEED TO BE A PROFESSIONAL to appreciate the subtleties of the chocolate experience. Much like a wine connoisseur at a wine tasting, chocolate lovers consider appearance, smell, and taste through a process we call The Five Senses of Chocolate.

To have a successful chocolate "tasting," there are a few basic tips to follow. If you are trying several varieties, neutralize your palate between each tasting. You can do this by eating a small piece of white bread, or sipping weakly brewed rose hip tea or water. Before tasting, do not eat any highly spiced foods.

The taste of the chocolate best develops at room temperature. It's important to begin the tasting with the chocolate with the lowest percentage of cocoa. Start with white chocolate, then milk chocolate, and finally dark chocolate. Gradually work up to higher-percentage varieties.

Chocolate is best tasted in a calm atmosphere so that you are able to concentrate on your senses. Before you take a bite, smell the chocolate, breathe in its aroma and take a good look at it. Is it shiny or dull? What is its color? Look at the texture of the chocolate bar; how does it break? Does it crumble and splinter or does it break cleanly with a hard and clear cracking sound? If it breaks with a distinct snap, it's usually the first sign of excellent quality. Does it begin to melt if you hold it between your fingers a few seconds? If it doesn't, it may contain a lot of vegetable fat that melts at higher temperatures than cocoa butter—not a sign of a premium product such as Lindt. The melting point of cocoa butter is just below body temperature so high cocoa butter content can actually feel cool on the tongue.

In the following we will explain the main principles.

THE FIVE SENSES

LOOK

Examine the chocolate's appearance—color, structure, and sheen. Premium chocolate like Lindt's should have a silky matte sheen and even texture. The color can run from deep, dark brown to auburn, or in the case of white chocolate, from pale ivory to yellow. The color is a result of the types of cacao beans. White chocolate will become increasingly yellow when more cocoa butter is added.

The sheen is a result of proper tempering. Tempering (see page 39) is a process that puts the cocoa butter crystals in perfect alignment. Proper handling and storage are also key in the appearance of chocolate (see page 33 for storage instructions).

A streaky white surface is the result of the cocoa butter crystals coming out of alignment and rising to the surface of the chocolate. This is referred to as "fat bloom" and indicates that the chocolate was improperly tempered, improperly stored, or is old.

TOUCH

Premium chocolate should have a smooth and silky feel, not rough or grainy. Such a surface can indicate poor conching or poor storage. If chocolate is stored in a high humidity environment it can develop a condition known as "sugar bloom," which is caused by condensation forming on the surface of the chocolate and the sugar rising to the top. The water evaporates and the sugar crystals remain on the surface, resulting in a gritty texture in your mouth during the melt.

LISTEN

Holding it close to your ear, break a piece of chocolate. Pay attention to the noise it makes; it may be distinct or dull. High-quality, unfilled chocolate breaks with a distinctly audible snap. The edge of the break should be smooth and without crumbs. This test confirms proper tempering and storage.

SMELL

You'll find that you can distinguish a wide range of aromas in chocolate. When you hold the piece of chocolate near your nose and breathe in deeply, resist the obvious impulse to say that it smells like chocolate and try to identify other aromas: red fruit, caramel, vanilla, spices, honey, earth—there are no wrong answers. Like wine grapes and coffee beans, some of the cacao bean's flavor will reflect the region in which it was grown, including qualities of the soil.

TASTE

Now for the best part! Tasting chocolate is the ultimate sensory experience. Let a piece melt slowly in your mouth and allow it to spread over your tongue. Does it melt smoothly, or does it leave a granular or pasty feeling in your mouth? Graininess indicates improper conching or too much sugar. Premium chocolate should not stick to your palate. It should have a fine texture and a soft melting quality. Over-sugaring chocolate not only produces a grainy texture, it can cause thirst as well.

Does it melt easily and change effortlessly from solid to liquid, without chewing? If it doesn't, it's too dry; but the opposite, fatty, will just leave that kind of taste in your mouth. An artfully created chocolate has a fine texture, a sensuous rather than fatty consistency, and softer melting qualities.

A high cocoa content, however, is no guarantee for flavor; it's the quality of the beans and the way they are processed and used in production that have the biggest impact on a chocolate product's final taste.

As the chocolate melts, try to discern the unique flavors other than the cocoa. Look for notes of vanilla, fruit, licorice, spices, and even tobacco. Premium chocolate will also linger in your mouth and the flavors will evolve.

ENJOY

A chocolate tasting event makes a wonderful theme for a get-together with friends. The simplest recipe in this book is this: Select a wide variety of Excellence bars, add family and friends, a festively entertaining environment, and savor true *Lindt Chocolate Passion.*

You will notice that Lindt chocolate will melt in your hand. This is also a sign of premium chocolate! Cocoa butter melts around body temperature. If you are handling a piece of chocolate that is not melting in your hands it indicates the use of other plant fats.

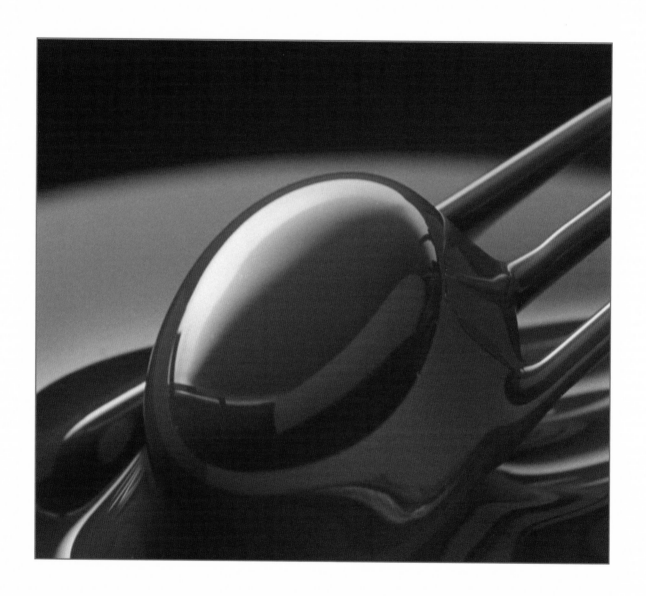

CHOCOLATE IS AN INCREDIBLY VERSATILE ingredient, and cooking with it is fairly straightforward, and most importantly, delicious. The process gets more complex, however, when the chocolate is to be used in its purest form.

WHAT IS TEMPERING?

Tempering is the process of building good, stable cocoa butter crystals in the complex system of chocolate. Accurate tempering ensures a beautiful shine on the surface and a clean snap when broken. If the chocolate is not tempered properly, the cocoa butter crystals rise to the surface of the chocolate and set as an unsightly white-gray film known as fat bloom. Although fat bloom doesn't affect the taste of chocolate, it results in a crumbly texture which might wind up with an inferior "mouth feel" and influences the chocolat's resistance to temperature.

Tempering is in any case very important, espcially when using chocolate for creations where the chocolate is visible, such as hand-rolled truffles, molded chocolates, or garnishes. For the recipes in this book, you'll need to temper the chocolate for anything that is finished by dipping in chocolate (florentines, macaroons, and dipped fruit), for finishing truffles, and for the bark recipes. Here the tempering process is required to get the best results from high quality chocolate such as Lindt.

WORKING WITH CHOCOLATE

3 STEPS TO TEMPER CHOCOLATE

Tempering needs to be done in a cool environment, with temperatures not exceeding 68°F (20°C). The humidity should be below 50 percent. There are various methods for tempering chocolate by hand, and they all involve three basic steps: (1) melting, (2) cooling, and (3) re-heating. The only critical piece of equipment required is a thermometer, and digital is best. If you choose to temper using the traditional method, and you don't have a marble slab, you would be wise to invest in one. Marble is the best material for controlling temperature when working with chocolate, so it's a worthwhile expense. You'll also need a scraper with which to push the chocolate around, and an offset metal spatula.

The first step is to chop or grate the chocolate (see page 45 for suggestions). Reserve a third of the chopped chocolate for adding during the cooling stage.

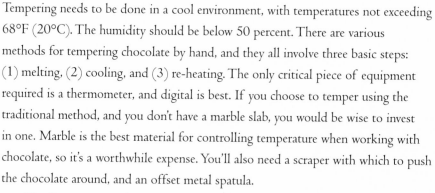

1
TEMPERING:
Melting Chocolate

IN ORDER TO MELT all of the crystals in the cocoa butter, gently heat the finely chopped chocolate to 118°F (48°C). Reaching these temperatures is crucial to the tempering process because there are several types of fat crystals in cocoa butter that melt at different temperatures. The most stubborn of the group will be completely melted only at 118°F (48°C). Using a digital thermometer during the process is the only way to be sure that this happens.

There are several ways of melting chocolate, and any of these methods can be used also for chocolate recipes that don't require tempered chocolate: It's important to *not* cover the saucepan or bowl with a lid, otherwise you risk condensation and thus moisture getting into the melting chocolate.

- **Double boiler.** This is the easiest and best method—one saucepan that holds the chocolate fits snugly into another that contains about an inch of simmering water. Make sure the water in the bottom pan never boils. The water should just begin to simmer. If you don't have a double boiler, you can use the next method: a bain-marie, or water bath.

- **Water bath (bain-marie).** This process requires care to ensure that no moisture will get into the chocolate or it will seize, or clump.
  You will need a medium-sized saucepan and a heat-proof bowl that fits tightly onto the rim of the saucepan. Place approximately 2 cups or 5

deciliters of water in the saucepan and bring to a gentle simmer, ensuring that the water never boils—you don't want the rising steam to condense and drip into the chocolate. Put the chopped chocolate into the bowl and place that on the saucepan. Frequently stir the chocolate until it is completely melted and then, while monitoring with a digital thermometer, warm the chocolate until it just reaches 118°F (48°C), and take the bowl off the saucepan.

- **Conventional oven.** You can melt chocolate in a dry oven by putting the chopped or grated chocolate in a metal bowl and placing that in an oven set at 110°F (43°C). If your oven cannot be set that low, use the lowest temperature and keep the door ajar. The chocolate will melt in about an hour or less.

- **Microwave oven.** This is more suitable for smaller quantities of chocolate. Place the finely chopped chocolate in a microwave-safe bowl. Place the bowl in the microwave and melt the chocolate in short intervals (approximately 15–20 seconds on 75 percent power), stirring after every interval. Once all the chocolate is molten, monitor the temperature with a thermometer.

THERE ARE ALSO SEVERAL WAYS OF cooling chocolate. The goal is to bring down the temperature of the molten chocolate to 81°F (27°C). Here is a time-saving tip: Warm a bowl by running it under hot water and then dry it thoroughly. Pour the chocolate into this warm bowl, and then proceed with one of the following methods:

2

TEMPERING:
Cooling Chocolate

- **Seeding process.** Add ⅓ of the total chocolate weight, finely chopped or grated, into the ⅔ of melted chocolate at 118°F (48°C). For example, if the total weight of the chocolate used in the recipe is 10.5 ounces (300 grams) of Lindt Excellence, that would require three 3.5-ounce/100-gram bars; melt two of them and then mix in one finely chopped bar. Stir the chocolate thoroughly and allow it to stand for a few minutes, so the temperature of the molten chocolate can slowly melt the finely chopped bar. Resume stirring until all the chocolate is melted and the temperature has reduced to approximately 81°F (27°C).

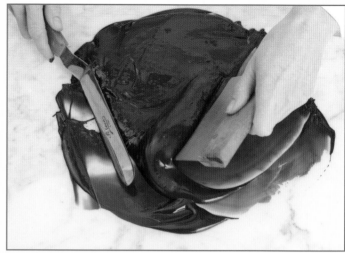

The classic method for tempering chocolate.

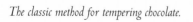

- **The traditional method.** Pour ⅔ of the molten chocolate (118°F/48°C) onto a marble slab and spread out with an offset metal spatula. Using a scraper, push the chocolate to the center; this will distribute the good crystals that are beginning to form. Mix the chocolate in the center and then spread it out again. Continue the process until the chocolate starts to set slightly. Once the chocolate has reached the consistency of pudding, add it back into the bowl containing the remaining one third of the melted chocolate and stir thoroughly. Check that the temperature is approximately 81°F (27°C).

WHILE CONSTANTLY MONITORING the temperature, gently heat the chocolate—dark chocolate to 90°F (32°C), milk couverture to 88°F (31°C), and white couverture to 86°F (30°C). In this phase the unstable crystals melt whereas the good crystals remain. The chocolate is now tempered. Before commencing work with the chocolate, take a small sample to check how the chocolate is setting. Just dip one corner of the spatula into the chocolate, place it somewhere out of the way on the kitchen counter, and allow it to set. If tempered correctly, it should set within a couple of minutes, with a nice, even shine.

3

TEMPERING:
Reheating Chocolate

GANACHE

Getting comfortable with making *ganache* can help you master an enormous range of luxurious recipes. Ganache is basically a complex emulsion-suspension of chocolate and cream. By changing some ingredients, proportions, and techniques, you can use ganache as a glaze or frosting, as truffles or a tart, or turn it into a warm drink, mousse, or a frozen confection.

The proportion of chocolate and cream determines the density of the finished ganache; more cream makes it lighter and more fluid, more chocolate makes it denser. You can also manipulate ganache by heating it to thin and cooling it to thicken.

You can use either whipping or heavy cream to make ganache, but each contains differing amounts of butterfat, which will affect the richness of the ganache. The higher the fat content of the cream, the richer the ganache will be.

The three basic factors involved in making ganache are (1) ingredients, (2) temperature, and (3) the method of mixing.

1

GANACHE:
Ingredients

THE TRICK WITH GANACHE IS THAT YOU'RE MIXING—or emulsifying—fat and water, and it is well known that oil and water don't mix. The cocoa butter in the chocolate is the fat, and the water is in the heavy cream. In order to emulsify them, you work with what they have in common: fat. The cream, heated to between 90°F (32°C) and 110°F (43°C), melts the chopped chocolate, so that the cocoa-butter fat can be stirred into tiny droplets suspended alongside the butterfat in the cream.

2

GANACHE:
Temperature

THE MORE CONSISTENT AND CONTROLLED the temperature of the ganache, the smoother it will be. That means you need to be patient while stirring and monitor the temperature with a digital thermometer. If the temperature gets too high, fat droplets will pool together and rise to the surface, separating from the mixture, which in this condition is referred to as "broken" (see "Repairing Broken Ganache").

You can avoid getting lumpy ganache by making sure the chocolate is chopped into very fine pieces, smaller than ¼ inch, before combining it with the hot cream. Repair lumpy ganache by reheating it.

3

GANACHE:
Mixing

AFTER COMBINING THE CREAM with the chocolate to melt the cocoa butter, the mixture is set aside to warm for a minute, and then stirred in a slow, circular motion. The stirring movement must be steady to reduce the fat to tiny droplets. If you stir too vigorously the temperature of the fat can fall below 90°F (32°C) too quickly, producing ganache with a grainy texture.

You can also make ganache in a food processor. Chop the chocolate into manageable pieces for the machine, and use the blade attachment in the food processor to finely grind the chocolate. Heat the cream, and while the machine is running, pour it in through the opening at the top of the processor. Process a few seconds until the ganache is smooth.

A classic ganache can generally stay at room temperature for two days, as long as it's kept in a cool place. If it's in a bowl, always place a piece of plastic wrap

firmly against its surface so a film or a sugar crust does not form on its surface.
Freeze for up to 3 months.

REPAIRING BROKEN GANACHE

If your ganache separates and becomes "broken," it is possible to repair it, although
this can be difficult to do and sometimes it's just better to start over. To repair
the ganache, divide it in half. Warm one half in a double boiler to 130°F (54°C).
This will melt the fat, making the mixture thinner. Cool the remaining ganache to
60°F (16°C) by stirring it over a bowl of ice. The fat in this portion will begin to
solidify, causing the ganache to thicken. When both halves have reached the desired
temperatures, slowly pour the hot ganache into the cold, and stir. If you want
to use a food processor for this step, you can put the cool ganache into the food
processor's bowl, turn on the machine, and pour in the warm ganache. Combining
the two portions of ganache this way helps to redistribute the temperature while re-
suspending the fat evenly in the water.

OTHER TECHNIQUES

For making chocolate curls, you can use a vegetable peeler—the type with a long,
narrow blade, and a chunk or bar of chocolate. Leave the chocolate out where it
can warm a little, while you warm the peeler blade slightly by running it under hot
water. Water will make the curl flake so be sure to dry the peeler before pulling it
along the chocolate's surface.

Making Chocolate Curls

When grating chocolate, a good food processor can be invaluable. Use the grating
attachment of the blade to process the chopped chocolate until it is finely ground.
You can use a hand grater, as well. Chill the chocolate and rub it against the grater's
large holes. If the chocolate is warm, it will smear and clog the grater.

Grating Chocolate

Recipes from the Lindt Maîtres Chocolatiers

RECIPE PHOTOGRAPHY BY JIM SCHERER
FOOD STYLING BY CATRINE KELTY

Truffles

CHOCOLATE TRUFFLES ARE LUXURIOUS small confections created from rich ganache, a combination of chocolate and cream. They can be rolled in cocoa powder, chopped nuts or chocolate or double dipped in tempered chocolate. Truffles are perfect for beginning to learn how to handle chocolate because they are easy to make and the result is so gratifying that you'll be encouraged to venture further on your chocolate exploration and try more complex recipes.

Believed to have originated in France, the truffle was named for the highly valued fungus of the same name. The original chocolate truffles were hand rolled and coated in cocoa powder, which gave them a striking visual similarity to their earthy namesake.

The recipes included in this section are for three basic types of truffle—milk, dark, and white chocolate. By using different methods for flavoring the ganache and finishing the truffles, you can create your own signature truffle to share with friends and family.

INTRODUCTION TO THE TRUFFLE RECIPES

FLAVORING TRUFFLE GANACHE

USE THE FOLLOWING METHODS to flavor the truffle ganache in the three basic recipes included in this section.

Liqueurs, Brandies, and Other Spirits

Replace ⅓ of the cream with your choice of liqueur, brandy, or liquor (see suggestions below). In the recipes in this book, that would mean replacing 1⅓ tablespoons of cream with the alcohol. Add the alcohol after the chocolate has completely melted in the cream. Suggested pairings:

- Kahlúa® or Baileys® with milk chocolate truffles
- Bacardi® White Rum with white chocolate
- Amaretto, whiskey, or cognac with dark chocolate

Tea & Coffee

Let the tea steep in the heated cream. For the recipes in this book, use 1 tea bag and let it steep for 3–5 minutes. Remove the tea bag and reheat the cream before combining it with the chocolate. You can also use a teaspoon of loose tea leaves. Strain after 3–5 minutes. Suggested pairings:

- Black tea with dark chocolate truffles
- Chai with milk chocolate truffles
- Herbal tea with white chocolate truffles

To make mocha truffles, use instant coffee. For the recipes in this book, use ½ teaspoon and add it to the hot cream. Whisk until it is dissolved. Suggested pairing:

- Mocha with dark chocolate truffles

Spices

By using the cream to make an infusion of your chosen spice or fruit, you can introduce exotic yet delicate flavor to your truffles. "Infusion" is a traditional term for brewing tea. Place the spice in the cream and heat it until it just comes to a boil. Remove from heat and set aside. The longer the spices are in the cream the stronger the flavor will be. For the recipes in this book, use small amounts (½ a cinnamon stick, ¼ teaspoon of lavender, 1 star anise, 2 cardamom pods). You can also use ½ teaspoon of peeled and chopped ginger root, chili, lemon, lime or orange peel. Strain the cream to remove the spices, herb, or fruit, and reheat before combining it with the chocolate. Suggested pairings:

- Cinnamon, star anise or cardamom with milk chocolate truffles
- Lavender or lime with white chocolate truffles
- Orange, ginger or chili with dark chocolate truffles

Fruit

For the recipes in this book, stir 1½ teaspoons of concentrated puree (found at specialty stores) into the cream prior to adding it to the chocolate. Suggested pairings:

- Raspberry, strawberry or lemon with white chocolate truffles
- Orange or raspberry with dark chocolate
- Cherry or banana with milk chocolate

FINISHING THE TRUFFLES

Easy

Finishing the truffles can be as simple as rolling them in cocoa powder or powdered sugar. You can also roll them in the following:

- Chocolate shavings, chopped chocolate
- Chopped toasted nuts: walnuts, pistachios, almonds, hazelnuts
- Coconut

After hand-rolling the truffles, place them on a shallow tray filled with the desired coating. Roll the truffle in the coating with either a pair of spoons or your hands.

Intermediate

The second option is to roll the truffles in tempered chocolate. Temper a few ounces of the desired type of chocolate. Wash your hands, rinse them in cold water and then dry them. Cold hands keep the truffle from softening as well as the tempered chocolate from getting too warm. Place a tablespoon of tempered chocolate in the palm of your hand and roll the truffles to coat. Place the finished truffle on a tray lined with parchment paper. Replenish the chocolate in your hands as needed. You can also roll the chocolate-coated truffles in cocoa powder or powdered sugar to finish.

   When tempering chocolate or working with tempered chocolate, the temperature of your work space is important. The temperature should not be above 70°F (21°C) or the chocolate might not set. Store truffles in a cool place. You can put them in the fridge, but they will sweat and potentially bloom when removed from the cold environment. Truffles are best enjoyed at room temperature.

Truffles will melt in your hands when you are rolling them, so try to work quickly and don't over roll. Use your fingertips and, when washing your hands, rinse them with cold water. You may also roll the truffles using cocoa powder to coat your hands. This will, however, only allow you to use one finish on the truffle (i.e. cocoa powder rather than chopped nuts or enrobing them in melted chocolate).

MILK CHOCOLATE TRUFFLES

WITH THEIR SUPER CREAMINESS and mild flavor, milk chocolate truffles are extremely popular with kids of all ages. Try rolling them in a finish of finely-chopped almonds, peanuts, or crushed toffee. You can also experiment with combining different kinds of Lindt milk chocolate by using tempered Swiss Classic Milk for the finish.

Ingredients

Ganache

¼ cup (60 milliliters) heavy cream

5 ounces (150 grams) Lindt Milk Chocolate, chopped

1 tablespoon (15 grams) butter, softened

Method

- Heat the cream until it just comes to a boil, add the chopped chocolate, and remove the saucepan from the heat.
- Stir or whisk the mixture until the chocolate is completely melted.
- Stir in the butter until the ganache is smooth.
- Put the ganache in a bowl and cover with plastic wrap, ensuring that the plastic makes contact with the entire surface of the ganache.
- Refrigerate overnight or until the ganache is set.

To form basic truffles

- Use a melon baller, small ice cream scoop, teaspoon, or piping bag.
- Roll the ganache in a ball and place on parchment paper.
- Roll finished truffles in unsweetened cocoa powder (see "Finishing the Truffles" on page 53 for more decorating tips).

Yield

Makes approximately 20 truffles.

Maîtres Chocolatiers

Ann Czaja & Hans Mazenauer

DARK CHOCOLATE TRUFFLES

DARK CHOCOLATE LOVERS will find that these make a perfect complement to an after-dinner cup of coffee or espresso, or glass of port.

Ingredients

> Ganache
>> ¼ cup (60 milliliters) heavy cream
>>
>> 5 ounces (150 grams) Lindt Bittersweet Chocolate, chopped
>>
>> 1 tablespoon (15 grams) butter, softened

Method

- Heat the cream until it just comes to a boil, add the chopped chocolate, and remove the saucepan from the heat.
- Stir or whisk the mixture until the chocolate is completely melted.
- Stir in the butter until the ganache is smooth.
- Put the ganache in a bowl and cover with plastic wrap, ensuring that the plastic makes contact with the entire surface of the ganache.
- Refrigerate overnight or until the ganache is set.

To form basic truffles

- Use a melon baller, small ice cream scoop, teaspoon or piping bag.
- Roll the ganache in a ball and place on parchment paper.
- Roll finished truffles in unsweetened cocoa powder (see "Finishing the Truffles" on page 53 for more decorating tips).

Yield

Makes approximately 20 truffles.

Maîtres Chocolatiers

Ann Czaja & Hans Mazenauer

Have you ever tried chocolate with a glass of wine? Whoever dares to try this experiment will discover a new passion because dark chocolate can be tasted in the same way as great wines. Both form a wonderfully harmonious blend if they are specially selected to go together.

WHITE CHOCOLATE TRUFFLES

THE WHITE CHOCOLATE TRUFFLE provides a lovely canvas for colorful finishes such as green and red sugar crystals for the winter holidays, but also subtle, elegant ones such as shredded coconut, finely-chopped hazelnut, and crystallized sugar shown here.

Ingredients

Ganache

¼ cup (60 milliliters) heavy cream

5 ounces (150 grams) Lindt White Chocolate, chopped

Method

- Heat the cream until it just comes to a boil, add the chopped chocolate, and remove the saucepan from the heat.
- Stir or whisk the mixture until the chocolate is completely melted.
- Stir in the butter until the ganache is smooth.
- Put the ganache in a bowl and cover with plastic wrap, ensuring that the plastic makes contact with the entire surface of the ganache.
- Refrigerate overnight or until the ganache is set.

The delicately flavored cocoa butter in this confection is a perfect vehicle for exotic flavors such as vanilla, tropical fruit flavors, and liqueurs such as the hazelnut-based Frangelico®, or almond-flavored amaretto.

To form basic truffles

- Use a melon baller, small ice cream scoop, teaspoon or piping bag.
- Roll the ganache in a ball and place on parchment paper.
- Roll finished truffles in unsweetened cocoa powder (see "Finishing the Truffles" on page 53 for more decorating tips).

Yield

Makes approximately 20 truffles.

Maîtres Chocolatiers

Ann Czaja & Hans Mazenauer

Bark, Fruit, and Fondue

ABOUT BARK

BARK IS SIMPLE TO MAKE—its resemblance to the rough surface of tree bark is part of its charm, but its main attraction is its versatility.

The different types of barks that can be created are probably endless. We have developed 3 distinct recipes using dark, milk, and white chocolate. Because Lindt chocolate is made with cocoa butter, it must be tempered when making these recipes.

WHITE CHOCOLATE BARK WITH PISTACHIOS & DRIED CRANBERRIES

RED CRANBERRIES AND GREEN PISTACHIOS embedded in white chocolate make this bark especially festive for the winter holidays.

Break bark irregularly, or, using a large knife, cut into more uniform pieces.

Ingredients

4 bars (3.5 ounces/100 grams each) Lindt Swiss Classic White Chocolate, chopped

½ cup (40 grams) pistachios

½ cup (60 grams) dried cranberries

Method

- Temper the chocolate according to the instructions on pages 40–43.
- Add the pistachios and dried cranberries to the tempered chocolate. Stir to combine.
- Spread the mixture on a baking tray lined with parchment paper.
- Refrigerate for 5–10 minutes, remove, and let set in a cool place.
- Store in an airtight container, in a cool place.

Yield

Approximately 1 pound (500 grams) of bark.

Maître Chocolatier

Ann Czaja

WHITE CHOCOLATE BARK WITH PEPPERMINT AND DARK CHOCOLATE DRIZZLE

CREAMY WHITE CHOCOLATE, blushing with refreshing peppermints, and laced with bittersweet chocolate, makes a classic confection. Wrapped in cellophane tied off with colorful ribbon, these make perfect holiday treats.

Ingredients

> 4 bars (3.5 ounces/100 grams each) Lindt Swiss Classic White Chocolate, chopped
> 1 cup (180 grams) Star Mints (individually wrapped red & white peppermints), crushed

> Drizzle
> ½ bar (1.75 ounces/50 grams) Lindt Bittersweet Chocolate

To crush the mints, unwrap and put them in a freezer bag, cover with a kitchen towel, and tap with a hammer.

Break bark irregularly, or, using a large knife, cut into more uniform pieces.

Method

- Temper the chocolate according to the instructions on pages 40–43.
- Add the crushed mints to the white chocolate. Stir to combine.
- Spread on a baking tray lined with parchment paper.
- Refrigerate for 5–10 minutes, then remove.
- Drizzle tempered dark chocolate over the white bark.
- Let set in a cool place.
- Store in an airtight container, in a cool place.

Yield

Approximately 1¼ pounds (560 grams) of bark.

Maître Chocolatier

Ann Czaja

WHITE CHOCOLATE BARK WITH DRIED APRICOTS

This bark makes an exquisite companion to an aperitif of amaretto.

THIS BARK COMBINES the tangy aroma and flavor of the dried apricot with the subtle cocoa-vanilla velvetiness of Lindt's Swiss Classic White Chocolate, preserving the essence of summer in fruit suspended in cream.

Ingredients

4 bars (3.5 ounces/100 grams each) Lindt Swiss Classic White Chocolate, chopped

1 cup (160 grams) dried apricots, chopped in large pieces

Method

- Temper the chocolate according to the instructions on pages 40–43.
- Add the chopped dried apricots to the tempered chocolate. Stir to combine.
- Spread the mixture on a baking tray lined with parchment paper.
- Refrigerate for 5–10 minutes, remove, and let set in a cool place.
- Store in an airtight container, in a cool place.

Yield

Approximately 1¼ pounds (560 grams) of bark.

Maître Chocolatier

Ann Czaja

MILK CHOCOLATE BARK WITH ALMONDS & RAISINS

Ingredients

4 bars (3.5 ounces/100 grams each) Lindt Swiss Classic Milk Chocolate, chopped
½ cup (80 grams) slivered almonds
½ cup (75 grams) raisins

Method

- Temper the chocolate according to the instructions on pages 40–43.
- Add the slivered almonds and raisins to the tempered chocolate. Stir to combine.
- Spread on a baking tray lined with parchment paper.
- Refrigerate for 5–10 minutes, remove, and let set in a cool place.
- Store in an airtight container, in a cool place.

Bark makes a great gift for any occasion, cut into bar-sized pieces, tied with colorful string or ribbon, and packed with festive tissue paper in a decorative box or tin.

DARK CHOCOLATE BARK WITH ALMONDS

Ingredients

4 bars (3.5 ounces/100 grams each) Lindt Bittersweet Dark Chocolate, chopped
1 cup (70 grams) whole almonds

Method

- Follow the directions above, using dark chocolate, and substituting the whole almonds for the slivered almonds and raisins.

Yield

Each recipe yields approximately 1 to 1¼ pounds (450–555 grams) of bark.

Maître Chocolatier

Ann Czaja

MILK CHOCOLATE BARK WITH PECANS & DRIED PEACHES

Ingredients

4 bars (3.5 ounces/100 grams each) Lindt Swiss Classic Milk Chocolate, chopped

½ cup (75 grams) pecans, chopped

½ cup (70 grams) dried peaches, chopped

Method

- Temper the chocolate according to the instructions on pages 40–43.
- Add the pecans and dried peaches to the tempered chocolate. Stir to combine.
- Spread on a baking tray lined with parchment paper.
- Refrigerate for 5–10 minutes, remove, and let set in a cool place.
- Store in an airtight container, in a cool place.

Capture two great tastes of the southern U.S.—the sweet, buttery flavor of pecans melded with peaches—in silky milk chocolate.

MILK CHOCOLATE BARK WITH DRIED BLUEBERRIES

Ingredients

4 bars (3.5 ounces/100 grams each) Lindt Swiss Classic Milk Chocolate, chopped

1 cup (230 grams) large dried blueberries

Method

- Follow the directions above, substituting the dried blueberries for the pecans and dried peaches.

Yield

Each recipe yields approximately 1¼ to 1⅓ pounds (550–630 grams) of bark.

Maître Chocolatier

Ann Czaja

DARK CHOCOLATE BARK WITH CAYENNE PEPPER & DRIED CHERRIES

THE DRIED CHERRIES lend a concentrated flavor to this dark chocolate creation. Look for the subtle "bite" of the cayenne as the chocolate finishes melting in your mouth.

Ingredients

4 bars (3.5 ounces/100 grams each) Lindt Bittersweet Dark Chocolate, chopped

1 cup (130 grams) dried cherries

1-2 teaspoons cayenne pepper

Method

- Temper the chocolate according to the instructions on pages 40–43.
- Add the dried cherries and cayenne pepper. Stir to combine.
- Spread on a baking tray lined with parchment paper.
- Refrigerate for 5–10 minutes, remove, and let set in a cool place.
- Store in an airtight container, in a cool place.

Yield

Approximately 1⅛ pounds (430 grams) of bark.

Maître Chocolatier

Ann Czaja

The amount of cayenne pepper is strictly to taste. 2 teaspoons is the recommended maximum for this recipe.

Break irregularly, or, using a large knife, cut into more uniform pieces.

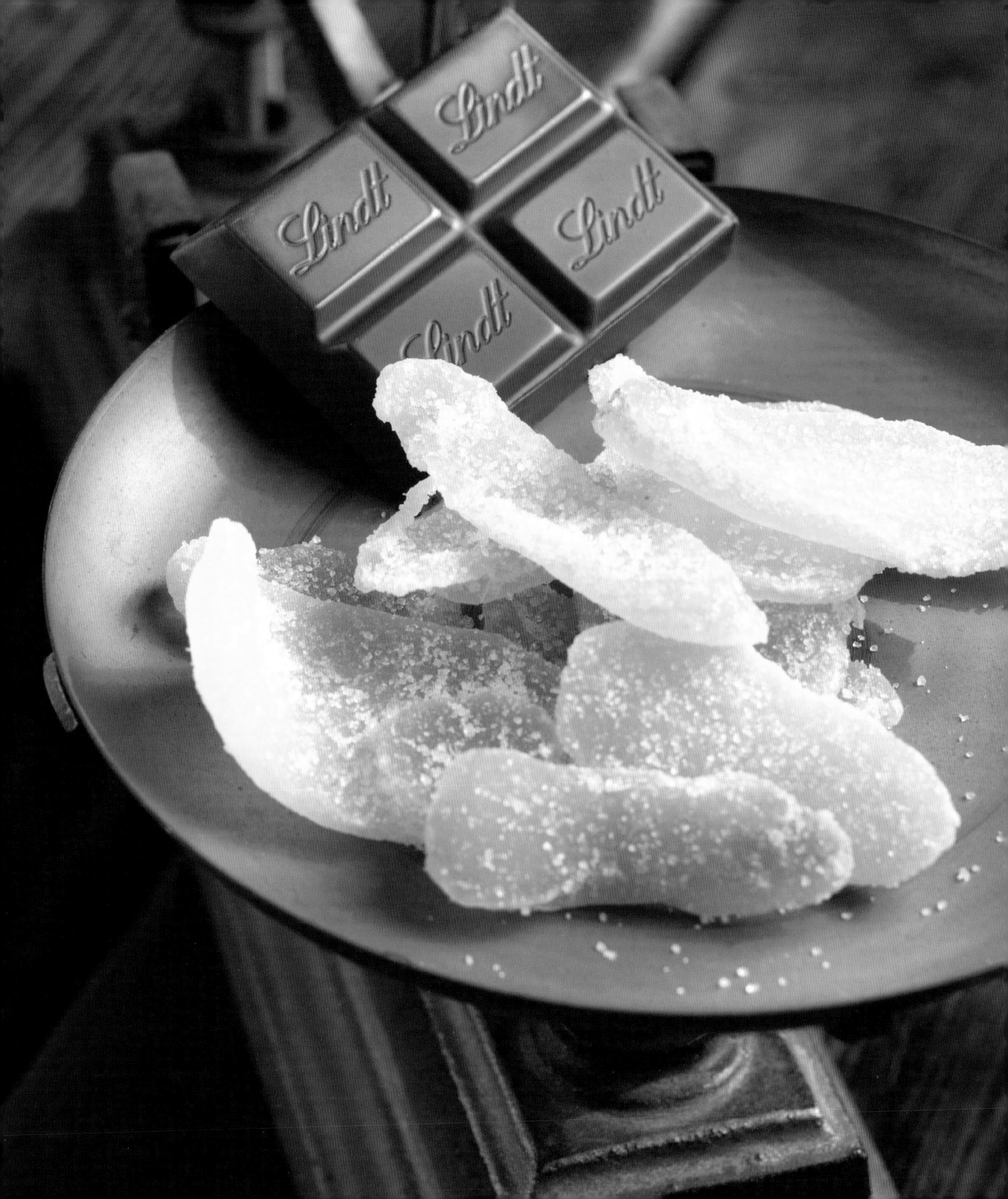
Lindt
Lindt
Lindt
Lindt

DARK CHOCOLATE BARK WITH CANDIED GINGER

DARK CHOCOLATE IS ONE OF THE FEW flavors strong enough to stand up to the sassy and spicy ginger. This is a wonderful treat to have on a cold day, when you need the comfort of dark chocolate and spicy ginger to warm you up inside.

Ingredients

4 bars (3.5 ounces/100 grams each) Lindt Bittersweet Dark Chocolate, chopped
½ cup (60 grams) candied ginger

Method

- Prepare the ginger by wiping off the excess sugar and chopping into small pieces.
- Temper the chocolate according to the instructions on pages 40–43.
- Add the ginger to the tempered chocolate and stir to combine.
- Spread on a baking tray lined with parchment paper.
- Refrigerate for 5–10 minutes, remove, and let set in a cool place.
- Store in an airtight container, in a cool place.

Ginger has long been known for its medicinal properties, particularly its ability to settle the stomach. This dark chocolate bark would make an elegant final course to a formal dinner.

Yield

Approximately 1 pound (450 grams) of bark.

Maître Chocolatier

Ann Czaja

CHOCOLATE FONDUE

THE ONLY THING MORE NOURISHING to the body and soul than a pot full of Lindt chocolate fondue is sharing it with your friends and family, and everyone's favorite dipping foods. Once you try it, you'll wonder how you ever lived without a fondue pot.

Ingredients

One bar (3.5 ounces/100 grams) Lindt Dark Chocolate, chopped
One bar (3.5 ounces/100 grams) Lindt Milk Chocolate, chopped
⅔ cup (160 milliliters) cream (heavy, light or half & half)

Accompaniments

- Pound cake cut into cubes
- Fresh fruit: grapes, strawberries, bananas, apples, pears, pineapple
- Dried fruit: apricots, pineapple, peaches, papaya, mango
- Marshmallows

Method

- Prepare your selection of dipping foods by cleaning and slicing as needed.
- Arrange dipping food on one or several platters according to your dinner or party plans, and reserve in the refrigerator.
- In a saucepan, heat the cream just until it starts to boil.
- Remove the saucepan from the heat and add the chopped chocolate. Stir until melted.
- Pour the chocolate mixture into the fondue pot and set on the table, with the platter(s) of dipping food, where everyone can comfortably reach it.

You can do an all dark or all milk chocolate fondue.

Brush apples and pears with a bit of lemon juice diluted in water. This will allow you to prep in advance and avoid brown fruit!

Yield

4 servings.

Maître Chocolatier

Ann Czaja

CHOCOLATE DIPPED STRAWBERRIES

Chocolate dipped strawberries have a very short life span! Dip them as close to serving time as possible.

Store in a cool place.

THE ULTIMATE CHOCOLATE and fruit pairing. This recipe is a fun activity to do with children, or a perfect addition to a romantic celebration.

Ingredients

3 bars (3.5 ounces/100 grams each) Lindt Bittersweet or White Chocolate, chopped

12–14 medium sized strawberries

Garnish

½ bar Lindt Bittersweet and/or White Swiss Classic Chocolate, for contrast, chopped

Method

- Wipe the strawberries with a damp cloth and pat dry. Do not wash them.
- Temper the chocolate according to the instructions on pages 40–43.
- Hold the strawberry by its green cap, and dip into the tempered chocolate.
- Gently shake off the excess chocolate and place the strawberry on a tray lined with parchment paper. Repeat with remaining strawberries.
- Place the tray in the refrigerator for about 5 minutes to set the chocolate.
- Using a piping bag with a small tip, drizzle with the contrasting chocolate onto the strawberry for a very elegant, professional look.

Variations

Take strawberries and other fresh fruits (kiwi, pineapple, melon, banana) and cut them into bite-size pieces. Put them on wooden skewers and place on a tray lined with parchment paper. Fill a small piping bag with tempered chocolate and drizzle it over the fruit kebabs. You can also drizzle the chocolate with a teaspoon. Handle like the dipped strawberries.

Yield

Approximately 12–14 medium strawberries.

Maître Chocolatier

Ann Czaja

CHOCOLATE DIPPED DRIED FRUIT

Make this fruit the same day you want to serve it.

Store in a cool place.

FRUIT DIPPED IN CHOCOLATE is a deliciously simple and elegant treat. Let your personal preferences guide you whether to use dark or white chocolate.

Ingredients

> 3 bars (3.5 ounces/100 grams each) Lindt Bittersweet or White Chocolate, chopped
>
> About 12 ounces (336 grams) of dried pineapple, papaya, mango, apricots, banana chips

Garnish
> ½ bar Lindt Bittersweet and/or White Chocolate, for contrast, chopped

Method

- Temper the chocolate according to the instructions on pages 40–43.
- Dip the dried fruits into the tempered chocolate.
- Gently shake off the excess chocolate and place the pieces of fruit on a tray lined with parchment paper.
- Place the tray in the refrigerator for about 5 minutes to set the chocolate.
- Using a piping bag with a small tip, drizzle with the contrasting chocolate.

Yield

12 ounces of dipped fruit, enough for 4–6 servings.

Maître Chocolatier

Ann Czaja

Mousse, Crème, and Parfait

CHOCOLATE MOUSSE

IF YOU LOVE TO ENTERTAIN, you'll want to make this recipe part of your basic repertoire. It is one of the easiest mousse recipes to make and stores well in the refrigerator a day in advance. Milk chocolate lovers, do not despair! Replace the dark chocolate with equal amounts of Lindt Milk Chocolate (Lindt Swiss Classic, Excellence Extra Creamy).

Ingredients

3 bars (3.5 ounces/100 grams each) Lindt Excellence 70% Cocoa Dark Chocolate, chopped

1 tablespoon (15 grams) butter

2 tablespoons (30 milliliters) hot water

1 tablespoon (15 milliliters) orange liqueur (optional)

2 cups (475 milliliters) heavy cream

4 egg yolks

¼ cup (50 grams) sugar

Only use the freshest eggs when making this recipe.

For a less intense mousse replace the 70% with Lindt Bittersweet Chocolate.

Try folding 2 teaspoons of coarsely ground black pepper into this intense mousse after adding the cream. The dark chocolate and pepper complement each other beautifully.

Garnish with white chocolate curls.

Method

- Melt the chopped chocolate and butter (see melting techniques on page 40).
- Add the hot water and orange liqueur to the chocolate and stir to form a smooth paste. Set aside.
- In a separate bowl, whip the cream until just barely firm. Set it aside in the refrigerator.
- In a separate bowl, whip the egg yolks and sugar.
- Add the chocolate to the egg yolks and stir until combined.
- Carefully fold in the whipped cream.
- Pour into a bowl or individual serving cups, cover with plastic wrap, and refrigerate a minimum 6 hours or overnight.

Yield

8–10 servings.

Maître Chocolatier

A combined effort from all our Maître Chocolatiers

WHITE CHOCOLATE MOUSSE

SERVED IN AN ELEGANT GLASS, white chocolate mousse is the epitome of subtle elegance. This recipe calls for egg whites to make the mousse extra light and fluffy, so it's of the utmost importance to use only fresh eggs.

Ingredients

3 bars (3.5 ounces/100 grams each) Lindt Swiss Classic White Chocolate, chopped

½ cup (120 milliliters) water, warm

2 cups (475 milliliters) heavy cream

4 egg whites

Method

- Melt the chopped chocolate (see melting techniques on page 40).
- When melted, stir in the water, and keep stirring until smooth. Set aside.
- In a separate bowl, whip the cream until firm and fold it into the chocolate ganache.
- In a clean, dry bowl, whip the egg whites until stiff, and carefully fold into the chocolate mixture.
- Pour into a bowl, or individual serving cups, and cover with plastic wrap.
- Refrigerate a minimum of 6 hours or overnight.

Yield

8–10 servings.

Maître Chocolatier

Ann Czaja

Replace ½ of the water with white rum.

Try adding a tablespoon of poppy seeds into the ganache to add delightful color and texture to the mousse.

Serve with whipped cream, fresh fruit, chocolate sauce, fruit coulis.

For an equally elegant presentation use a hot tablespoon to form a quenelle of mousse, place it on a chilled dessert plate, and decorate with the garnishes mentioned above.

STRACCIATELLA MOUSSE

FOR THIS CHOCOLATE-CHIP inspired dessert, be sure to use the Lindt Excellence 85% Cocoa bar. You'll also want to use the freshest eggs when making this recipe. Stracciatella mousse can easily be made without rum; simply replace the alcohol with hot water.

Ingredients

3 bars (3.5 ounces/100 grams each) Lindt Swiss Classic White Chocolate, chopped

1 bar (3.5 ounces/100 grams) Lindt Excellence 85% Cocoa Dark Chocolate, chopped

3 tablespoons (45 milliliters) rum

2 cups (475 milliliters) heavy cream

4 egg yolks

Method

- Melt the chopped white chocolate (see melting techniques on page 40), add the rum and stir until a smooth paste is formed. Add a little hot water if the paste is too stiff. Set aside.
- In a separate bowl, whip the cream and reserve it in the refrigerator.
- In a separate bowl, whip the egg yolks.
- Add the white chocolate to the egg yolks and mix until combined.
- Fold in the whipped cream.
- Fold in the chopped dark chocolate.
- Place in a bowl or individual serving dishes and cover with plastic wrap.
- Refrigerate a minimum of 6 hours or overnight.

Yield

8–10 servings.

Maître Chocolatier

Ann Czaja

Only use the freshest eggs when making this recipe.

The classic garnish for this dessert is the mint leaf, shown here, but you can also use a hot tablespoon to shape a large quenelle of mousse and place it on a chilled dessert plate. Serve with a "mirror" of chocolate sauce or raspberry coulis (strained berry puree sweetened with powdered sugar), or serve with a dollop of whipped cream.

CINNAMON MOUSSE

THIS MOUSSE IS VERY FESTIVE, and it may turn into your new holiday favorite. Serve it garnished with fresh raspberries and topped with a Lindt Thin.

Ingredients

2 cups (475 milliliters) heavy cream

3 bars (3.5 ounces/100 grams each) Lindt Swiss Classic White Chocolate, chopped

2 tablespoons (30 milliliters) water, hot

2 tablespoons (30 milliliters) rum (can replace with same amount of water)

2 teaspoons ground cinnamon

4 egg yolks

Method

- Whip the cream and reserve it in the refrigerator.
- Melt the chocolate (see melting techniques on page 40). Stir in hot water, rum, and cinnamon. If the paste is too stiff, add a bit more water or rum and continue stirring until it reaches a smooth consistency. Remove from the heat and reserve.
- In a separate bowl, whip the egg yolks.
- Stir chocolate mixture into eggs.
- Fold in the reserved whipped cream.
- Refrigerate in a serving bowl or individual serving cups a minimum of 6 hours or overnight. Make sure you cover the mousse completely with plastic wrap.

Only use the freshest eggs when making this recipe.

Try replacing the white chocolate with Excellence Extra Creamy Milk Chocolate for a Chocolate Cinnamon Mousse.

Yield

8–10 servings.

Maître Chocolatier

Ann Czaja

MADAGASCAR RED WINE MOUSSE

THIS MOUSSE HAS AN UNUSUAL flavor combination that you will not soon forget. The mildness of Lindt's Madagascar 70% Cocoa, with its cinnamon-citrus notes, is a perfect complement to the complex flavors in a strong red wine such as Barolo (Italian), Rioja (Spanish), or Bordeaux (French).

Ingredients

2 bars (3.5 ounces/100 grams each) Lindt Excellence Madagascar 70% Cocoa Dark Chocolate, chopped

¾ cup (180 milliliters) heavy cream

½ cup (180 milliliters) strong red wine

1–2 tablespoons powdered sugar (optional)

Add the optional powdered sugar while you are whipping the chilled mixture if you desire a sweeter mousse.

Method

- Pour the cream into a saucepan and bring to a simmer. Remove from heat and stir in the chopped chocolate.
- Add the red wine and stir.
- Pour the mixture into a bowl, cover with plastic wrap, and refrigerate a minimum of 6 hours or overnight.

To Serve

- Whip the chilled mixture as you would whip cream.
- The best way to serve this mousse is to pipe it on Lindt Thins. Using a pastry bag and a star tip, pipe rosettes of the mousse onto the thins. Serve with a glass of red wine.
- Or, serve in a chilled martini glass. Pour a bit of chocolate sauce (see page 93) in the glass and, using a spoon or piping bag, place the mousse in the glass. Garnish with a sprig of fresh mint and a square of Madagascar chocolate.

Yield

6–8 portions, piped on Lindt Thins or served traditionally.

Maître Chocolatier

Hans Geller

PANNA COTTA WITH CHOCOLATE SAUCE

THE ORIGINAL ITALIAN SUPERSTAR. Panna cotta is a traditional rustic dish and is very easy to make. Unlike other custard-like desserts, it contains no egg and is a great way to showcase a fine dairy product, set like a gem in a ring of chocolate sauce.

Ingredients

> 3 teaspoons unflavored gelatin
>
> 1 cup (240 milliliters) whole milk
>
> 2 cups (475 milliliters) heavy cream
>
> ¼ cup (50 grams) sugar
>
> 1 vanilla bean, sliced lengthwise or 1 teaspoon vanilla extract
>
> Chocolate Sauce (see page 93)

Method

- Pour the milk into a small bowl, sprinkle the gelatin over the milk, and set aside to let it soften.
- Combine the cream, sugar, and vanilla bean or extract in a saucepan and, stirring continuously, bring to a heavy simmer over medium-low heat.
- Remove from heat.
- Remove the vanilla bean, scrape out the remaining seeds, and return them to the cream.
- Add the gelatin/milk mixture and whisk.
- Pass this mixture through a strainer into a large measuring cup or bowl to remove any undissolved gelatin or bits of vanilla bean.
- Pour into ramekins, and cool completely.
- Cover with plastic wrap and refrigerate a minimum of 6 hours or overnight.

To Serve

- Unmold (see page 93) and serve with Chocolate Sauce.

Serve with a "mirror" of chocolate sauce, fresh strawberries and mint sprig or pour the sauce directly over the panna cotta.

A mint chocolate sauce would also complement the flavor of the panna cotta.

CHOCOLATE SAUCE

Ingredients

2 tablespoons (15 grams) cornstarch

⅓ cup (35 grams) cocoa powder

1 cup (240 milliliters) water

1 ¼ cup (250 grams) sugar

2.6 ounces (75 grams) Lindt Bittersweet Dark Chocolate, chopped

Method

- Mix the cornstarch and cocoa powder in heat-proof bowl. Add enough cold water to make a smooth paste.
- Combine the water and sugar in saucepan and, on medium heat, bring to a slow boil. Stir in the chopped chocolate.
- Whisk until the chocolate is completely melted.
- Whisk the hot liquid into the cornstarch and cocoa paste until incorporated and return to the saucepan.
- Whisking continuously, allow the sauce to come to a slow boil for 1 minute.
- Strain the sauce through a sieve.
- Sauce can be served warm or cold. Place plastic wrap directly on the surface of the sauce to prevent the formation of "skin." Store in the refrigerator up to 2 weeks.

Assembly

To unmold:

- Dip the ramekin into hot water to release the panna cotta or run a small, thin knife around the edge to loosen.
- Turn the ramekin upside down onto a dessert plate.
- Hold the plate and bottom of ramekin and shake gently to release.
- Carefully remove ramekin and serve with chocolate sauce.

Yield

6–8 servings.

Maître Chocolatier

Ann Czaja

MILK CHOCOLATE AND CARDAMOM PANNA COTTA

THE TRADITIONAL ITALIAN DESSERT gets a new and exotic twist with milk chocolate and cardamom.

Ingredients

3 ½ teaspoons unflavored gelatin

⅔ cup (160 milliliters) milk

7 cardamom pods

2 ½ cups (600 milliliters) heavy cream

⅓ cup (65 grams) sugar

9 ounces (250 grams) Lindt Excellence Extra Creamy Milk Chocolate, chopped

Method

- In a small bowl, sprinkle the gelatin over the milk and set aside.
- On a chopping board, slightly bruise the cardamom pods with the blade of a knife in order to release their aroma.
- Place the cardamom pods in a saucepan along with the cream and sugar. Bring the liquid to a boil and remove from heat. Strain out the cardamom pods, and return liquid to the saucepan.
- Add the chocolate to the hot cream and whisk until completely melted. Add the milk/gelatin and whisk until the gelatin is dissolved. Strain the mixture into a bowl.
- Pour the mixture into ramekins and refrigerate at least 6 hours or overnight.
- Cover with plastic wrap when cooled completely.
- Unmold as described on page 93 and serve the Panna Cotta with coulis (as shown here) or a cherry compote, such as the one featured on page 193.

You could easily substitute the cardamom with cinnamon, vanilla or even rose petals.

To make coulis, blend and strain fresh or frozen berries and pass through a sieve. Sweeten to taste with powdered sugar.

Yield

8–10 servings in 4-ounce (120-milliliter) ramekins.

Maître Chocolatier

Thomas Schnetzler

WHITE CHOCOLATE CRÈME BRÛLÉE

BREAK THE SUGAR CRUST and savor the creamy custard that awaits you.

Ingredients

5 egg yolks

⅓ cup (65 grams) sugar

Pinch of salt

2 cups (475 milliliters) heavy cream

One bar (3.5 ounces/100 grams) Lindt Swiss Classic White Chocolate, chopped

Sugar to caramelize, approximately 1 teaspoon per ramekin

Serve Crème Brûlée as is or with a small decoration of fresh fruit on one side (fresh berries, mint sprig).

Method

- Preheat oven to 300°F (150°C).
- Place 6 ramekins in a heat-proof baking pan, deep enough to fill with water to middle of ramekin.
- Whisk egg yolks, sugar, and salt together in a heat-proof bowl.
- Heat heavy cream to a light simmer and add chopped chocolate; stir or whisk until the chocolate is completely melted.
- Slowly pour the hot cream into egg yolk mixture, whisking continuously.
- Strain and pour the liquid into the ramekins waiting in the baking pan and place that on the oven rack in oven. Fill the baking dish with hot water until it reaches the middle of the ramekins. This method prevents water from "sloshing" into the crème brûlée mixture.
- Bake 30–35 minutes.
- Remove from oven, let cool, and refrigerate. The recipe can be made the day before serving.
- Caramelize just before serving (see page 100).

Yield

6 servings, in six 4-ounce (120-milliliter) ramekins.

Maître Chocolatier

Ann Czaja

MILK CHOCOLATE AND COCONUT CRÈME BRÛLÉE

Under-fill the ramekins rather than over-filling them.

THIS VERY RICH CRÈME BRÛLÉE will satisfy the coconut lover in you. If you prefer, you can decrease the amount of coconut cream used and replace it with cream.

Ingredients

1 ¼ cups (400 milliliters) coconut cream

1 ¾ cups (425 milliliters) heavy cream

8 egg yolks

5 ounces (150 grams) Lindt Excellence Extra Creamy Milk Chocolate, chopped

2 tablespoons (30 milliliters) coconut rum

Sugar to caramelize, approximately 1 teaspoon per ramekin

Method

- Preheat oven to 250°F (120°C).
- Pour the coconut cream and heavy cream into a saucepan and bring to a boil over moderate heat.
- Place the egg yolks in a heat-proof bowl.
- Once the cream reaches the boiling point, remove from the heat and pour approximately ¼ of it over the egg yolks and whisk vigorously. This will prevent the egg yolks from curdling.
- Place the chopped chocolate in a heat-proof bowl and pour the remaining cream over it. Stir until completely melted and the mixture is smooth.
- Add the egg yolk mixture and the coconut rum to the chocolate mixture, and whisk until smooth.
- Divide the brûlée mix equally into the ramekins and place them into a deep baking dish.
- Place the baking dish with ramekins into the oven. Pour enough boiling water into the baking dish to reach halfway up the ramekin sides.
- Bake approximately 40 minutes or until just set. A brûlée is cooked when the custard is set on the sides, but remains slightly soft in the center.
- Caramelize just before serving (see page 100).

Yield

8 servings in eight 4-ounce (120-milliliter) ramekins.

Maître Chocolatier

Thomas Schnetzler

ABOUT BRÛLÉE

Crème brûlée can be caramelized up to 2 hours before serving and returned to the refrigerator. To achieve the distinct, crunchy finish on top of a crème brûlée, sprinkle an even layer of sugar on top of the dessert and using a brûlée torch (available at kitchen stores) caramelize the sugar until golden brown. Hold the torch just above the top of the ramekin, and make sure you do not put the flame directly on the sugar.

You can also use your broiler to achieve this affect. Place the ramekins on a baking sheet, and place it on the topmost rack beneath the broiler. If using a broiler, make sure the ramekins are rotated to prevent uneven caramelization. Watch them closely; they will caramelize quickly.

SPICED RICOTTA CREAM WITH BALSAMIC STRAWBERRIES

FRESH RICOTTA CHEESE imbued with softly delectable Madagascar chocolate, dressed with balsamic vinegar-soaked strawberries, this Italian inspired dessert is a very "rustic" dish.

Ingredients

Zest of one orange

2 cloves

1 cinnamon stick

½ cup (100 grams) sugar

⅔ cup (160 milliliters) water

One bar (3.5 ounces/100 grams) Lindt Excellence Madagascar 70% Cocoa Dark Chocolate, chopped

1 cup (250 grams) ricotta cheese

Pinch of salt

Method

- In a saucepan, combine the orange zest, cloves, cinnamon stick, sugar, and water. Bring to a boil over medium heat. Cook about 10 minutes until the liquid forms a thick syrup. Remove from the heat and let cool.
- Melt the chocolate (see melting techniques on page 40). Let cool.
- Strain the syrup into a mixing bowl.
- In a large bowl, mix the ricotta, salt, and the syrup until combined. Add the melted chocolate.
- Place in a serving bowl and refrigerate for 2–3 hours.

"Zest" is the most colorful part of a citrus rind, and full of aromatic oil. Use either a zester or the small holes on a hand grater to lightly scrape off the zest. A light touch will help avoid taking the bitter white pith along with the zest.

BALSAMIC STRAWBERRIES

½ pint (100 grams) fresh strawberries, cleaned and cut into quarters

2 tablespoons balsamic vinegar

¼ cup (50 grams) sugar

Method

- Place the prepared strawberries in a bowl. Add the balsamic vinegar and sugar. Stir gently until combined.
- Cover and let them sit one hour at room temperature before serving. Do not leave fruit out for more than 4 hours.

Yield

4–6 servings.

Maître Chocolatier

Hans Geller

Using a tablespoon, place one good-sized quenelle on a chilled dessert plate and serve with a portion of the berries. Dust with powdered sugar if desired.

CHOCOLATE TIRAMISU

Tiramisu is traditionally made with lady fingers or a plain cake. The chocolate cake and chocolate shavings in this recipe add to its decadence.

VIVA ITALIA! Literally, *tiramisu* means "pull me up," a tribute to the effect of the coffee and alcohol-soaked cake that provides the structure for this dessert. This Tiramisu introduces chocolate to the traditional recipe.

Ingredients

Base

½ recipe of Basic Chocolate Cake (see page 145)
baked in an 8-inch (20-centimeter) square pan

Coffee to soak the cake

1 cup (125 milliliters) strong coffee

2 tablespoons (30 milliliters) marsala, coffee liqueur, or rum

Cream

3 egg yolks

⅓ cup (65 grams) sugar

8 ounces (226 grams) mascarpone

1 tablespoon (15 milliliters) marsala, coffee liqueur, or rum

1 cup (125 milliliters) heavy cream

Method

- Whip the egg yolks and sugar until fluffy.
- Add the mascarpone and the desired alcohol. Beat until smooth.
- Whip the heavy cream and fold into the mascarpone mixture.

Assembly

For one pan:

- Cut the cake in half horizontally and soak with ½ of the coffee mixture.
- Spread half of the mascarpone mixture evenly across the cake.
- Repeat with second half of cake and remaining mascarpone mixture.
- Cover and refrigerate 6 hours or overnight.

Only use the freshest eggs when making this recipe.

For individual glasses:

■ Cut the cake into cubes and follow the above method. Depending on the size of the glass you may do three layers rather than two.

To Serve

Cover the top of the Tiramisu with chopped or shaved dark chocolate. Sprinkle with cocoa powder. To serve the large Tiramisu, cut into portions and remove with a spatula.

Yield

6 servings from one 8-inch (20-centimeter) square dish, or 6 individual glasses.

Maîtres Chocolatiers

Ann Czaja & Hans Geller

CHOCOLATE SOUFFLÉ GLACÉ GRAND MARNIER®

THIS AMAZING CHOCOLATE SOUFFLÉ is a classic dessert using Lindt Excellence 70% Cocoa Dark Chocolate. Serve this at your next dinner party for a taste experience that your guests will never forget.

Ingredients

2 cups (475 milliliters) heavy cream

2 ounces (60 grams) Lindt Excellence Intense Orange Dark Chocolate, chopped

2 eggs

¼ cup (50 grams) sugar

¼ cup (60 milliliters) Grand Marnier

Parchment paper cut in strips to wrap around the ramekins. This "collar" must be about an inch above the rim of the ramekin.

Method

- Prepare the ramekins. Cut the paper collars, wrap them around the individual ramekins, and secure them with tape. Set aside.
- Whip the cream and reserve in the refrigerator.
- Melt the chopped chocolate (see melting techniques on page 40). Set aside to cool.
- In a separate bowl, whip the eggs and sugar together.
- Add the melted chocolate to the eggs and sugar.
- Add the Grand Marnier.
- Fold in the whipped cream.

- Pipe or spoon the mixture into the prepared ramekins. Use a spatula or knife to smooth out the surface of the soufflé.
- Cover with plastic wrap and freeze overnight.

Serving Suggestions

- To serve, dust the top of the soufflé with cocoa powder and remove the collar. Place the ramekin on a dessert plate.
- You can substitute any Lindt dark chocolate for the Exellence Intense Orange.
- If using a chocolate other than Excellence Intense Orange, try substituting the Grand Marnier with amaretto or hazelnut liqueur (such as Frangelico®).

Servings

4–5 servings in 4-ounce (120-milliliter) ramekins.

Maîtres Chocolatiers

Ann Czaja & Hans Geller

Only use the freshest eggs when making this recipe.

CHOCOLATE PARFAIT

THIS SMOOTH, DARK AND creamy parfait is the perfect dessert on a warm evening.

Ingredients

½ cup (50 grams) slivered almonds, toasted

½ cup (50 grams) pistachios, toasted

2 cups (475 milliliters) heavy cream

1 egg

1 egg yolk

⅓ cup (65 grams) sugar

5 ounces (150 grams) Lindt Excellence 70% Cocoa, chopped

Optional:

¼ teaspoon chili powder

Method

- Line a 9 x 5-inch (23 x 13-centimeter) loaf pan (or rectangular cake pan) with plastic wrap, with enough extra length to fold over the pan.
- Toast the nuts in a skillet on the stove and set aside.
- Place ¼ of cream (½ cup) in a saucepan and bring to a boil.
- Remove from heat, stir in the chopped chocolate, and whisk until smooth. Set aside.
- Whip the egg, egg yolk, and sugar until light and fluffy. Fold in chocolate mixture and stir until smooth.
- In a separate mixing bowl, whip the cream until it is just firm and gently fold into the chocolate mixture
- Stir in the nuts (and chili powder, if desired).
- Pour the mixture into the prepared loaf pan, smooth the top with a spatula, and fold ends of the plastic over the top of the parfait.
- Freeze overnight.

Only use the freshest eggs when making this recipe.

Slice parfait and place on a chilled dessert plate. Accompany with fresh berries or cherry compote (such as the one featured on page 193) and a dollop of whipped cream.

To make individual parfaits, spoon the mixture into lined ramekins or molds.

Yield
Serves 8.

Maître Chocolatier
Thomas Schnetzler

CHOCOLATE POT DE CRÈME

THIS CLASSIC FRENCH DESSERT is a favorite of chocolate lovers worldwide.

Ingredients

6 ounces (180 grams) Lindt Bittersweet Chocolate, chopped

1 cup (240 milliliters) heavy cream

½ cup (125 milliliters) milk

¼ cup (50 grams) sugar

4 egg yolks

2 tablespoons (30 milliliters) orange liqueur

Method

- Combine the chopped chocolate, cream, milk, and sugar in a saucepan, double boiler, or over a simmering water bath (see melting techniques on page 40).
- Heat while stirring until chocolate is completely melted. Bring to a heavy simmer and remove from heat.
- Put the egg yolks in a heat-proof bowl and beat lightly. Add a small amount of the hot cream mixture to the yolks and stir. Pour cream/yolk mixture into the cream/chocolate and add the orange liqueur.
- Return the pan to the heat and stir until thickened (so that the chocolate mixture coats the back of a spoon).
- Pass the mixture through a sieve and pour into Pot de Crème cups or demitasse cups. Fill them ½ to ¾ full depending on size of cup.
- Refrigerate 4–6 hours or overnight. Cover with plastic wrap when completely cooled.

Only use the freshest eggs when making this recipe.

To garnish, place a dollop of whipped cream on the Pot de Crème. Dust with cocoa powder if desired.

Yield

6–8 servings.

Maître Chocolatier

Ann Czaja

Cookies and Brownies

DOUBLE CHOCOLATE MINT CHIP COOKIES

THESE COOKIES HAVE JUST the right balance of mint and dark chocolate. Subtly delicious!

Store these cookies in an airtight container to keep them fresh.

Ingredients

3 bars (3.5 ounces/100 grams each) Lindt Bittersweet chocolate, chopped

½ cup (114 grams) butter, softened

½ cup (100 grams) sugar

½ cup (90 grams) light brown sugar, firmly packed

4 eggs, lightly beaten

½ teaspoon mint extract

2 ¼ cups (235 grams) flour

1 teaspoon baking powder

½ teaspoon baking soda

½ teaspoon salt

2 bars (3.5 ounces/100 grams each) Lindt Excellence Intense Mint Dark Chocolate, chopped into small chunks

Method

- Melt the bittersweet chocolate according to instructions on pages 40–41.
- Cream together butter and sugars until light and fluffy.
- Reduce the mixer speed and add the eggs and mint extract.
- Stir in the melted chocolate.
- Sift the dry ingredients and add to the chocolate mixture.
- Stir in the chopped Excellence Intense Mint Chocolate.
- Let the dough rest in the refrigerator for 1 hour.
- Preheat oven to 350°F (180°C).
- Line cookie sheets with parchment paper. Spoon dough in rounded teaspoonfuls onto paper. Bake 12–15 minutes. Cool on wire rack.

Yield

About 4 dozen cookies.

Maître Chocolatier

Ann Czaja

CHOCOLATE NUT CLUSTERS

THIS RECIPE IS SIMPLE AND ELEGANT. Serve with coffee after your next dinner party or while gathered in the den for family night.

Ingredients

2.5 ounces (75 grams) hazelnuts or almonds, chopped, slightly toasted

One bar (3.5 ounces/100 grams) Lindt Bittersweet Dark or Lindt Swiss
    Classic Milk Chocolate

2.5 ounces (75 grams) walnuts, chopped, slightly toasted

Method

- Toast the nuts in a skillet over medium heat. Shake or stir continuously until the nuts start to turn golden brown. Transfer nuts to a bowl.
- Melt the chocolate (see melting techniques on page 40), then cool until the chocolate begins to set on the side of the bowl.
- Add the chopped nuts and mix well.
- Using a teaspoon, drop clusters of the mix onto a baking sheet lined with parchment paper.
- Allow to set in a cool place.

Substitute other nuts if desired. Toasting the raw nuts gives them a deeper, more concentrated flavor.

Yield

Approximately 16 clusters.

Maître Chocolatier

Hans Mazenauer

PEANUT BUTTER CHOCOLATE CHUNK COOKIES

FOR EVERYONE WHO LOVES chocolate in their peanut butter and vice versa.

Ingredients

½ cup (114 grams) butter, softened

½ cup (130 grams) chunky peanut butter

½ cup (100 grams) sugar

½ cup (90 grams) light brown sugar, firmly packed

1 egg, slightly beaten

1 teaspoon vanilla extract

1 ¼ cup (150 grams) flour

½ teaspoon baking powder

½ teaspoon baking soda

¼ teaspoon salt

2 bars (3.5 ounces/100 grams each) Lindt Bittersweet Chocolate, chopped in chunks

Try substituting Excellence Extra Creamy Milk Chocolate for the dark chocolate. It works equally well!

Method

- Preheat oven to 350°F (180°C).
- Line cookie sheets with parchment paper.
- Combine the butter, peanut butter, and sugars and cream together.
- Add the egg and vanilla extract.
- Combine the dry ingredients and add to the butter mixture.
- Stir in the chopped chocolate.
- Drop cookies by teaspoonfuls onto the prepared cookie sheets.
- Bake 10–12 minutes.
- Cool on a wire rack and store in an airtight container.

Yield

Approximately 3 dozen cookies.

Maître Chocolatier

Ann Czaja

OATMEAL SABLÉ

THE CLASSIC SABLÉ (pronounced "sah-blay") is rolled in sugar before it is baked. This recipe loses the sugar crust, but adds oatmeal and white chocolate. Drizzle with chocolate for a simple, but effective finish.

Ingredients

1 cup plus 1 tablespoon (210 grams) butter, softened

1 cup (100 grams) powdered sugar

1 teaspoon vanilla extract

1⅔ cup (220 grams) flour

¾ cup (70 grams) oats

1 tablespoon baking powder

½ bar (3.5 ounces/100 grams each) Lindt Swiss Classic White Chocolate, chopped

To decorate

½ bar (3.5 ounces/100 grams each) Lindt Swiss Classic Milk Chocolate

½ bar (3.5 ounces/100 grams each) Lindt Swiss Classic White Chocolate

Method

- Cream the butter, sugar, and vanilla extract.
- Add the flour, oats, and baking powder and mix until combined.
- Stir in the chopped white chocolate.
- Roll the dough into a log shape, wrap in plastic, and refrigerate at least 30 minutes.
- Preheat oven to 350°F (180°C).
- Cut cookies approximately ¼ inch (6 millimeters) thick and place them on a baking tray lined with parchment paper.
- Bake 15–20 minutes or until cookies just begin to brown slightly at the edges.
- Cool on a wire rack.
- When cookies are completely cooled, melt the milk or white chocolate and drizzle it over the cookies.

You can also use baking paper to shape the dough. Place the dough toward the center of one end of a large sheet of baking paper. Fold the farthest end of the paper over the dough and using a scraper or ruler push the paper under the dough.

You can decorate these cookies with a drizzle of milk chocolate, as shown, or with a combination of milk and white chocolate for a more dramatic effect.

Yield

Approximately 3 dozen cookies.

Maître Chocolatier

Urs Liechti

MILK CHOCOLATE MAPLE MACADAMIA COOKIES

THE SUBTLE TASTE OF MACADAMIA nuts and a touch of maple syrup complement each other in these tasty cookies.

Ingredients

⅔ cup (150 grams) sugar

2 tablespoons maple syrup

¾ cup (170 grams) butter

1 egg, beaten

2 ½ cups (180 grams) flour

¼ cup (40 grams) macadamia nuts, coarsely chopped

2 ounces (60 grams) Lindt Swiss Classic Milk Chocolate, chopped

This dough freezes well. Make a double batch and freeze one or two logs for emergencies!

Store in an airtight container to preserve freshness.

Method

- Combine the sugar, maple syrup, and butter and beat until creamy.
- Add the egg.
- Add the flour.
- Add the nuts and chocolate.
- Separate the dough into two portions and roll into 2 "logs." Use a little flour if necessary.
- Wrap in parchment paper or plastic wrap and let rest in the refrigerator for a minimum of 6 hours or overnight.
- Preheat oven to 350°F (180°C).
- Cut dough into approximately ¼-inch (6-millimeter) slices, and place on cookie sheets lined with parchment paper.
- Bake 10–12 minutes or until the cookies just begin to turn golden brown.

Yield

Approximately 30 cookies.

Maître Chocolatier

Urs Liechti

GANACHE FILLED ANISE MERINGUES

THESE DELICATE MERINGUES are so easy to make and yet look like the work of a master. Everyone appreciates the care that goes into these melt-in-your-mouth cookies, so take the praises you'll get, gracefully!

If you can't find ground anise, grind the seeds using a mortar and pestle or a spice grinder (a clean coffee grinder also works).

Anise can be omitted or substituted with other spices including allspice, cinnamon, nutmeg or pumpkin pie spice.

Ingredients

Meringue

    2 egg whites

    Pinch of salt

    ¾ cup (150 grams) sugar

    1 teaspoon anise seeds

Ganache

    5 ounces (150 grams) Lindt Bittersweet Dark Chocolate, chopped

    ½ cup (120 milliliters) heavy cream

    ½ teaspoon ground anise

    Cocoa powder to garnish

MERINGUE

Method

- Preheat oven to 320°F (160°C).
- Combine the egg whites and salt and beat until foamy.
- Gradually add the sugar, beating till the egg whites are stiff (will hold a peak) and glossy.
- Fold in the anise seeds.
- Put the meringue in a piping bag with a round tip.
- Pipe walnut sized rounds of meringue onto a cookie sheet lined with baking paper.
- Bake approximately 15 minutes, remove from oven, and let them cool on the baking paper.

GANACHE

Method

- Melt the chocolate and ⅓ of the cream over a water bath, stirring constantly.
- Remove the ganache from heat and let cool for 10 minutes.
- Beat the remaining cream until firm.
- Fold the whipped cream into the slightly cooled melted chocolate mixture.
- Stir in the ground anise.

Assembly

Shortly before serving:

- Take a small amount of the ganache and spread it on one half of a meringue.
- Repeat on a second half and sandwich together. You can also pipe the ganache onto the meringue with a pastry bag and small star tip.
- Dust finished meringues with cocoa powder and serve in paper confectioner cups.

Yield

Approximately 36 pieces, filled.

Maître Chocolatier

Ann Czaja

FLORENTINES

THESE DELICATE, LACY COOKIES are standard fare in fine European shops.

Ingredients

⅓ cup (70 milliliters) cream (heavy or half & half)

¼ cup (45 grams) sugar

2 tablespoons (30 grams) butter

1 tablespoon (25 grams) honey

¾ cup (70 grams) sliced almonds

⅓ cup (50 grams) candied fruit

2 tablespoons (15 grams) flour

One bar (3.5 ounces/100 grams) Lindt Bittersweet Dark Chocolate or
   Lindt Swiss Classic Milk Chocolate

Make sure the nuts and candied fruit are evenly dispersed and not clumped in the center; otherwise, the edges will bake faster and burn.

Store in an airtight container.

Serve with your favorite vanilla ice cream.

Method

- Combine the almonds, candied fruit, and flour in bowl.
- Place the cream, sugar, butter, and honey in a saucepan and cook over medium heat. Using a thermometer, bring cream mixture up to 237°F (114°C).
- Pour the cream mixture immediately onto the dry ingredients and gently mix together. Let the mixture cool slightly, but it should remain warm.
- Place small dollops (½–¾ teaspoon) of the mixture on baking trays lined with parchment paper. Leave a generous amount of space between the cookies because they will spread. Using a fork, press the cookies to flatten.
- Bake at 350°F (180°C) approximately 5 minutes or until golden brown.
- Remove from oven and let cool on the tray. Once set, transfer to a rack.
- When completely cooled, spread tempered chocolate on the bottom of the cookies. Turn them upside down to allow the chocolate to set.

Yield

Approximately 16 cookies.

Maître Chocolatier

Urs Liechti

CLASSIC CHOCOLATE BROWNIES

EVERYONE HAS THEIR FAVORITE brownie recipe and this is one of ours. The success of a brownie depends not only on the ingredients, but also on not overbaking it.

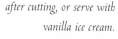

Dust with powdered sugar after cutting, or serve with vanilla ice cream.

Try using a bar of Lindt Excellence 70% Cocoa in place of one Bittersweet bar for a more intense brownie.

Substitute pecans or almonds for the walnuts.

Store in an airtight container.

Ingredients

3 bars (3.5 ounces/100 grams each) Lindt Bittersweet Chocolate, chopped
⅓ cup (75 grams) butter
3 eggs
¾ cup (150 grams) sugar
1 teaspoon vanilla extract
½ teaspoon salt
1 cup (120 grams) flour
1 cup (150 grams) chopped walnuts

Method

- Preheat oven to 350°F (180°C).
- Grease an 8 x 8-inch (20 x 20-centimeter) square baking pan and line with parchment paper.
- Melt the chopped chocolate and butter (see melting techniques on page 40). Stir constantly.
- Remove from the heat and let cool slightly.
- Beat together the eggs, sugar, vanilla, and salt until well combined.
- Add the melted chocolate, and beat gently by hand or on a low setting on a mixer until evenly incorporated.
- Add the flour and walnuts, and mix until just combined.
- Pour the mixture into the prepared pan and bake approximately 20 minutes.

Yield

Approximately 25 small brownies.

Maître Chocolatier

Ann Czaja

CHOCOLATE, ALMOND & ORANGE BROWNIES

Warm the brownies slightly before serving. This will enhance the fragrance of the Intense Orange chocolate.

THIS UNIQUE BROWNIE IS PERFECT for any occasion. Serve it at room temperature to enjoy its rich orange flavor.

Ingredients

⅔ cup (100 grams) slivered almonds

9 tablespoons (135 grams) butter

1 ⅓ cup (135 grams) powdered sugar

Zest of 1 orange

4 eggs, separated

1 ½ bars (150 grams) Lindt Excellence Intense Orange Chocolate, chopped

1 cup plus 2 tablespoons (135 grams) almonds, finely ground

⅓ cup (40 grams) flour

Pinch of salt

2 teaspoons (10 milliliters) orange liqueur (can substitute orange juice)

Chocolate Ganache frosting (optional) (see page 136)

Method

- Preheat oven to 340°F (170°C).
- Grease an 8 x 8-inch (20 x 20-centimeter) square baking pan and line with parchment paper.
- Toast the slivered almonds in a skillet over medium heat. Shake or stir continuously until the nuts start to turn golden brown. Transfer slivered almonds to a bowl and set aside.
- Combine the butter, sugar, and zest in a bowl and mix until light and pale.
- Add the egg yolks one at a time.
- Gently melt chopped chocolate over a water bath and add to the butter mixture. Scrape down sides of bowl to assure there are no lumps.
- Mix the ground almonds and flour, and fold into the chocolate mixture.
- Add the orange liqueur.

- In a dry, clean bowl, whip the egg whites with a pinch of salt until they form stiff peaks. Gently fold the whites into the chocolate mixture.
- Fold in the toasted almond slivers.
- Pour the batter into the prepared pan and bake approximately 30–40 minutes or until a toothpick inserted into the brownie comes out clean.
- Cool completely and frost with Chocolate Ganache. Cut into squares and serve.

Rather than frosting the brownie with the set ganache, pour the slightly warm ganache over the surface and spread..

CHOCOLATE GANACHE

1 bar (3.5 ounces/100 grams) Lindt Excellence 70% Cocoa Dark Chocolate, chopped
½ cup (120 milliliters) heavy cream
1 tablespoon (13 grams) sugar
1 tablespoon (15 grams) corn syrup
1 tablespoon (15 grams) butter, unsalted

Method

- Place the chopped chocolate in a heat-proof bowl.
- Combine the cream, sugar and syrup in a saucepan and bring to a boil over medium heat.
- Pour the hot liquid over the chocolate and stir until smooth.
- Stir in the butter.
- Cover the ganache with plastic wrap (make sure the plastic makes contact with the surface of the ganache) and set aside to cool.

Yield

8–10 brownies.

Maître Chocolatier

Thomas Schnetzler

CHOCOLATE PETITS FOURS

THESE BITE SIZED CAKES ARE AN ELEGANT alternative to cookies or brownies. Let your imagination guide you when you decorate them.

Ingredients

4.5 ounces (125 grams) Lindt Excellence 70% Cocoa Dark Chocolate, chopped

6 tablespoons (90 grams) butter

¾ to 1 cup (150–200 grams) granulated sugar

3 eggs, slightly beaten

3 tablespoons (20 grams) flour

3 tablespoons (20 grams) finely ground almonds

Petits fours forms

Petits fours forms can be found at fine kitchen stores and via the internet.

Method

- Preheat oven to 400°F (200°C), and grease the forms.
- Melt the chocolate, butter, and sugar in a double boiler. Remove from heat.
- Add the eggs, flour, and almonds. Stir until combined.
- Fill the petits fours molds ¾ of the way and, before baking, decorate with ingredients such as candied orange peel, candied fruits, chopped nuts, fresh pear cubes, raspberries, lemon or orange pulp. (See alternate method, below.)
- Bake for 10 minutes.

Variations

- Bake the petits fours ungarnished, then cool and decorate with colored sugar, powdered sugar, cocoa powder, candied violets, candied fruits, or fresh berries.
- Replace the 70% Excellence with Excellence Intense Mint dark chocolate or, for a mocha flavor, add instant coffee to the basic recipe.

Yield

Approximately one dozen, depending on the size and shape of your forms.

Maîtres Chocolatiers

Hélène Mazuyer, Jean-Pierre Larramendy, & David Vignau

CHOCOLATE DIPPED COCONUT MACAROONS

These chocolate dipped snow white cookies look and taste wonderful.

Ingredients

3 egg whites

¼ teaspoon salt

1 cup (200g) sugar

2 ½ cups (200g) flaked coconut

1 bar (3.5 ounces/100 grams) Lindt Bittersweet Chocolate, chopped

Method

- Line cookie sheets with parchment paper.
- Beat the egg whites and salt until foamy.
- Gradually add the sugar.
- Continue beating until the egg whites are glossy and form stiff peaks.
- Fold in the coconut.
- Drop in rounded teaspoonfuls or pipe mixture onto prepared cookie sheets.
- Let the cookie "dry" for 5–6 hours or overnight in a dry, non-humid area.
- Bake at 300°F (150°C) for approximately 10 minutes. They should just barely be golden brown on the tips.
- Cool completely on a wire rack.

These cookies are humidity sensitive. If they are dried in a room that is too warm and humid they will not maintain their shape in the oven.

As an option, sprinkle with powdered sugar before serving.

To Dip

- Melt the dark chocolate using tempering instructions (see page 40).
- Dip the base of each cookie into the dark chocolate and place on parchment paper.
- After the chocolate has set store in an airtight container.

Yield

Makes approximately 40 cookies.

Maître Chocolatier

Ann Czaja

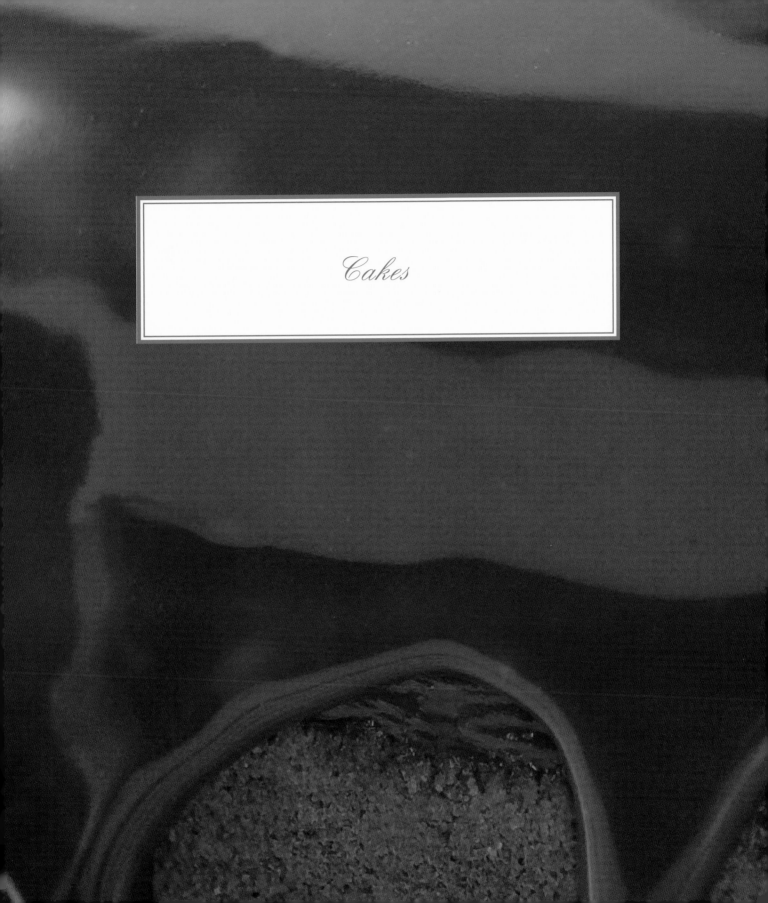

Cakes

BASIC CHOCOLATE CAKE

THIS VERSATILE CAKE can be used as the base for most of the recipes in this chapter. The manner in which the cake is mixed affects its volume and texture, so take care to mix the batter as instructed. When combining the dry ingredients with the wet, blend them smoothly in as few strokes as possible, to keep the texture of the cake light.

Ingredients

4.6 ounces (130 grams) Lindt Bittersweet Dark Chocolate, chopped

1 cup plus ½ tablespoon (120 grams) butter, softened

⅓ cup (40 grams) powdered sugar

Pinch of salt

6 eggs, separated

¾ cup plus 2 tablespoons (180 grams) sugar

¾ cup plus 2 tablespoons (130 grams) flour, sifted

This cake is the perfect base for making the Dark & Light Truffle Cake, Black Forest Cake, and Chocolate Layer Cake, all in this chapter.

Accurate measurement is important when baking cakes, so use measuring cups of the type of volume for which they were meant, for example, don't use fluid measuring cups for dry ingredients.

Method

- Preheat oven to 350°F (180°C). Grease baking pans and line the bottoms with parchment paper.
- Melt the chocolate according to instructions on page 40 and set aside.
- Cream butter, powdered sugar, and salt.
- Add the egg yolks one at a time to the butter mixture.
- Add the melted chocolate.
- Whip the egg whites, gradually adding the sugar and beating until stiff.
- Carefully fold ⅓ of the egg whites into the chocolate mixture.
- Fold in the remaining egg whites and sifted flour.
- Pour the batter into the baking pans and bake approximately 40 minutes. Baking time will decrease if using 2 cake pans. Check at 30 minutes. Cakes are done when a toothpick inserted in the center of the cake comes out clean.

Yield

One 9-inch (23-centimeter) springform, or two 8-inch (20-centimeter) cake pans, or two 9-inch (23-centimeter) cake pans. Makes 8–10 servings.

Maître Chocolatier

Hans Geller

CHOCOLATE LAYER CAKE

THIS MAKES A BEAUTIFUL birthday or special occasion cake.

Ingredients

1 recipe Basic Chocolate Cake (page 145)

Chocolate Butter Cream Frosting

16 ounces (450 grams) Lindt Bittersweet Dark Chocolate, chopped

⅓ cup (35 grams) cocoa powder

6 tablespoons orange juice or liquor (coffee liqueur, rum, cognac)

½ cup (50 grams) of powdered sugar

1 ½ cups (340 grams) butter, softened to room temperature

If using a springform pan you can also cut the cake in thirds, to create three layers.

For extra moistness make a simple syrup of 1 part water, 1 part sugar. Boil until the sugar dissolves. Add a tablespoon of orange liqueur or amaretto (optional). Brush the syrup on the layers before filling and frosting.

Method

- Make the cake according to the recipe.
- Melt the chocolate according to instructions on page 40. Set aside to cool to room temperature.
- Combine the cocoa powder and liquid to make a smooth paste, and set aside.
- Beat the sugar and butter until light and fluffy.
- Add the melted chocolate and beat until smooth.
- Add the cocoa paste and beat until smooth.

Assembly

- Turn cake layers upside down to ensure a flat surface (or cut a single cake in half to create two layers). Trim the bottom if necessary to ensure evenness.
- Spread frosting on bottom layer. Top with second layer.
- Spread frosting on top and sides of cake.

Yield

One 8- or 9-inch layer cake (20- or 23-centimeter) or one 9- or 10-inch springform cake (23- or 24-centimeter). Makes 8–10 servings.

Maîtres Chocolatiers

Hans Mazenauer & Ann Czaja

GERMAN CHOCOLATE CAKE

THIS CAKE IS POPULAR because of the variety of texture in the frosting that melts and crunches all at once into a rich and fragrant chocolate cake.

Ingredients

This recipe will make a three-layer cake. If that is too much for you then wrap the extra layer in plastic and freeze.

½ (120 milliliters) cup boiling water

1 bar (3.5 ounces/100 grams) Lindt Excellence 70% Cocoa Dark Chocolate, chopped

2 cups (400 grams) sugar

1 cup (228 grams) butter, softened

4 eggs, separated

1 teaspoon vanilla extract

2½ cups (275 grams) cake flour

1 teaspoon baking soda

1 teaspoon salt

1 cup (240 milliliters) buttermilk

Method

- Preheat oven to 350°F (180 C).
- Grease three round 8- or 9 ½-inch cake pans. Line the bottoms with parchment paper.
- Pour the boiling water over the chocolate in a small bowl, stirring until the chocolate is melted. Let cool.
- Mix the sugar and butter in a large mixing bowl until light and fluffy.
- Beat in the egg yolks one at a time.
- Beat in the chocolate and vanilla at low speed.
- Mix in the flour, baking soda, and salt alternately with buttermilk, beating after each addition until batter is smooth.
- Beat the egg whites until stiff, and fold into batter.
- Divide the batter among pans.
- Bake until a toothpick comes out clean: 8-inch layers 35–40 minutes, 9-inch layers 30–35 minutes. Let cool completely before frosting.
- Fill the layers and frost the cake with Coconut-Pecan Frosting (page 150).

COCONUT-PECAN FROSTING

Ingredients

    1 cup (200 grams) sugar

    1 cup (240 milliliters) evaporated milk

    ½ cup (114 grams) butter

    3 egg yolks

    1 teaspoon vanilla extract

    1 ⅓ cup (160 grams) coconut

    1 cup (150 grams) pecans, chopped

Method

- Mix the sugar, evaporated milk, butter, and vanilla in saucepan. Cook over medium heat, stirring occasionally, until thick, about 12 minutes.
- Stir in the coconut and pecans.
- Let the frosting cool. Stir before spreading on cake.

Yield

8–10 servings.

Maître Chocolatier

Ann Czaja

BLACK FOREST CAKE

THIS CAKE (SCHWARZWÄLDER KIRSCHTORTE) is traditionally made with Kirschwasser, a clear cherry brandy, which is added to the cherry liquid.

Ingredients

Cake

> 1 recipe Basic Chocolate Cake (page 145) baked in a 9- or 10-inch springform pan

Filling

> One 15-ounce can (425 grams) of dark cherries in sweet syrup (not pie filling)
>
> 2 cups (475 milliliters) heavy cream
>
> 2 tablespoons powdered sugar

Syrup

> Reserved liquid from cherries
>
> 1–2 tablespoons of cherry brandy or clear liqueur (optional)

Decoration

> One bar (3.5 ounces/100 grams) Lindt Bittersweet Dark Chocolate, or Lindt Excellence 70% Cocoa
>
> 10 to 12 cherries, fresh or reserved from the canned cherries

Method

- Make the cake, turn it upside down to cool, and cut in half horizontally. Trim bottom of cake to ensure that it sits flat and even.
- Drain the cherries and reserve the liquid. Add the alcohol to the liquid, if desired. Set aside.
- Whip the cream, add the powdered sugar, and set aside in the refrigerator.
- Chop or shave the dark chocolate. This will be used to decorate the finished cake.

Assembly

- Using a pastry brush or spoon, soak the bottom half of the cake with ½ of the cherry syrup.

- Spread a thin layer of the whipped cream onto the surface of the cake. Using a pastry bag with a round tip, pipe 3 rings onto the surface of the cake.

- Place the cherries in between the rings. Alternatively, this can be done by spreading a thick layer of cream on the surface and arranging the cherries in a circular pattern.

- Place the second half of the cake on top and press down lightly. Soak the top of the cake with the remaining cherry liquid.

- "Frost" the cake with the sweetened whipped cream, reserving enough to decorate the top with cream rosettes.

- Press the chopped/shaved dark chocolate onto the sides of the cake and sprinkle on the top surface.

- Pipe 8 to 10 cream rosettes on the top of the cake using a pastry bag and a star tip. Decorate with fresh or canned cherries.

Yield

One 9- or 10-inch (23- or 25-centimeter) springform pan makes 8–10 servings.

Maître Chocolatier

Hans Geller

MARBLE CAKE

Try substituting the loaf pan with an 8- or 9-inch square (20- or 23-centimeter) baking pan.

AN OLD STANDARD, marble cake reveals its dual nature when sliced.

Ingredients

1 ounce (30 grams) Lindt Excellence 85% Cocoa Dark Chocolate, chopped

1 ⅓ cups (300 grams) butter, softened

1 ½ cups (300 grams) sugar

5 eggs, separated

2 ½ cups (300 grams) flour

Method

- Preheat the oven to 350°F (180°C). Grease and flour the loaf pan.
- Melt the chopped chocolate (see melting techniques on page 40). Remove from heat and set aside.
- Whip butter; slowly add ⅔ of the sugar.
- Add the egg yolks to butter mixture.
- Sift the flour and gradually add to the butter mixture.
- Whip the egg whites, slowly adding remaining sugar, until they form stiff peaks.
- Fold the egg whites into the batter.
- Remove a little less than ½ of the batter and transfer to a bowl.
- Add the melted chocolate to the reserved smaller amount of batter and stir to incorporate.
- Spoon the batters, alternating the colors, into the prepared loaf pan.
- Smooth out the surface of the cake and, using a knife dipped in oil, score the center of the batter to ensure an even split on the surface during baking.
- Bake about 50 minutes or until a toothpick inserted into the center of the cake comes out clean. Remove from pan and cool on a wire rack.
- Dust with powdered sugar or cocoa powder before serving.

Yield

One 9 x 5 x 3-inch (23 x 13 x 8-centimeter) loaf pan, for 8–10 servings.

Maîtres Chocolatiers

Ann Czaja & Hans Geller

FLOURLESS TOFFEE, DATE, AND HAZELNUT CAKE

THIS RICH, MOIST CAKE also makes wonderfully decadent cupcakes.

Ingredients

10 large dates (220 grams)

⅔ cup (150 milliliters) water

3 tablespoons (45 milliliters) hazelnut liqueur (such as Frangelico®)

½ teaspoon vanilla extract (or ½ vanilla pod, split)

3 eggs

3 egg yolks

Pinch of salt

⅔ cup (120 grams) brown sugar

¾ cup (170 grams) butter

2 bars (3.5 ounces/100 grams each) Lindt Excellence Toffee Crunch, chopped

½ bar (3.5 ounces/100 grams each) Lindt Excellence 70% Cocoa Dark Chocolate, chopped

1⅔ cup (200 grams) hazelnuts, ground

⅔ cup (100 grams) hazelnuts, roasted, skinned, and chopped

For cupcakes, as shown on the facing page, line a cupcake pan with paper liners, and adjust the cooking time to approximately 20 minutes.

Try replacing the hazelnuts with almonds and the Frangelico with amaretto.

Method

- Preheat oven to 340°F (170°C). Grease a 9- or 10-inch (23- to 24-centimeter) springform pan and line the bottom with parchment paper.
- Roast the ⅔ cup hazelnuts in a shallow pan for 8–10 minutes; remove from oven and put on a kitchen towel. Fold towel over the nuts and allow to steam for 5 minutes. Rub vigorously in the towel. This procedure will remove most of the skin. Chop the nuts and set aside.
- Remove the pits from the dates and place them in a saucepan with the water, liqueur, and vanilla bean or extract.
- Simmer over low heat until the dates are soft; remove the vanilla bean. Remove the saucepan from the heat and push the mixture through a coarse sieve, creating a smooth puree. Set aside to cool.

- Beat eggs, yolks, salt, and brown sugar until the mixture is light and fluffy.
- Place the butter in another saucepan and melt over medium heat. Add the chopped chocolate. Remove from heat and stir until the chocolate is completely melted and the mixture is smooth.
- Mix the chocolate and butter into the whipped egg mixture. Fold in the date puree and ground hazelnuts, ensuring that there are no lumps. Mix until well incorporated.
- Stir in the chopped hazelnuts.
- Pour the batter into the prepared springform pan and smooth the top with the back of a spoon.
- Bake 40–50 minutes or until done (check with toothpick).
- Allow cake to cool in pan. Remove and top with ganache. (See "Chocolate Almond Orange Brownies" on page 136 for ganache recipe.)

Yield

One 9- or 10-inch springform pan (23- to 24-centimeter) for 8–10 servings, or twelve cupcakes.

Maître Chocolatier

Thomas Schnetzler

VIENNESE CHOCOLATE TORTE

THIS TORTE TAKES ITS INSPIRATION from the Viennese pastry chefs of the nineteenth century. The chocolate torte is one of the most famous cakes in the world and has been a favorite of chocophiles for generations.

Ingredients

Cake

⅔ cup (160 grams) butter, softened

5.7 ounces (160 grams) Lindt Bittersweet Dark Chocolate, chopped

2 cups (200 grams) powdered sugar

1 teaspoon vanilla extract

Pinch of salt

5 eggs, separated

¼ cup (50 grams) sugar

2 ⅓ cups (250 grams) flour

1 teaspoon baking powder

¾ cup plus 1 tablespoon (200 milliliters) milk

Filling

1 cup (240 grams) apricot jam, strained

Glaze

¾ cup plus 1 tablespoon (200 milliliters) heavy cream

2 bars (3.5 ounces/100 grams each) Lindt Bittersweet Chocolate, chopped

¼ cup (60 grams) butter

Ensure that the cake is completely covered with the apricot preserves. This step is important because it will cause the chocolate glaze to adhere to the cake and give it a smooth finish.

Serve a slice of the cake with a dollop of whipped cream.

Method

Cake

■ Preheat oven to 350°F (180°C). Grease, line with parchment, and flour a 10-inch (24-centimeter) springform pan.

■ Melt the butter and chocolate in a mixing bowl over a simmering water bath.

■ Remove from heat and add powdered sugar, vanilla, and salt. Beat until smooth and creamy.

■ Add the egg yolks one at a time.

- In a separate bowl, beat the egg whites, gradually adding the sugar until they form stiff peaks.
- Combine the flour and baking powder.
- Add the flour mixture and the milk to the butter/chocolate mixture. Do this in stages, beginning and ending with the flour mixture. Beat until smooth.
- Carefully fold in the egg whites.
- Pour batter into the prepared pan and bake 50–60 minutes. Use the toothpick method to test if the cake is finished.
- Turn the cake out onto a wire rack upside down and allow it to cool.
- Level out the cake on top (which is now the bottom) with a sharp knife. This step ensures that the cake will be even when it is finished.
- Cut the cake in half horizontally.

Apricot Filling
- Place the bottom ½ of cake on a wire rack placed on a baking sheet or tray. (You will need something to "catch" the run-off of the glaze, below.)
- Strain the apricot jam into a saucepan and warm over low heat.
- Spread some of the jam in the middle; not too much or the halves will slide instead of sticking together. Press the top half of the cake onto the bottom half.
- Pour the remaining preserves onto the top of the cake and spread evenly. Spread onto the sides of the cake as well.

This cake can also be made without the apricot filling and glaze. Try a ganache filling, as shown above, or perhaps a mousse. Finish with the chocolate glaze.

Chocolate Glaze
- Heat the cream in a saucepan, add the chopped chocolate, and stir until it is completely melted.
- Stir in the butter.
- Pour the glaze over the cake liberally. The glaze should envelop the entire cake.
- Place the cake "as is" in the refrigerator to set. Before serving transfer to a cake plate and let stand at room temperature for about 20 minutes.
- Cut with a warm, sharp knife.

Yield

One 10-inch (24-centimeter) round cake for 8–10 servings.

Maître Chocolatier

Flora Grösslich

GUGLHUPF WITH CHOCOLATE

THIS IS A VERY POPULAR CAKE in Europe. The special Guglhupf form gives it a distinctive shape.

Ingredients

1 cup (250 grams) butter, softened

2 ½ cups (250 grams) powdered sugar

1 teaspoon vanilla extract

¼ teaspoon salt

4 eggs

2 ½ cups (250 grams) flour

1 tablespoon baking powder

1 bar (3.5 ounces/100 grams) Lindt Bittersweet Chocolate, finely chopped

1 teaspoon cocoa powder

1 teaspoon cinnamon

½ cup (125 milliliters) milk or red wine

Method

- Preheat oven to 350°F (180°C). Grease and flour a 9- or 10-inch (23- or 25-centimeter) Guglhupf form.
- Beat the butter, sugar, vanilla extract, and salt until creamy and nearly white.
- Add the eggs one at a time. The butter mixture may separate when the eggs are added, but will bind with the addition of the dry ingredients.
- Mix the dry ingredients together, including the finely chopped chocolate.
- Add the dry ingredients and the milk (or red wine) to the butter mixture. Add alternately, beginning and ending with the dry ingredients.
- Put the batter in the form and bake 50–60 minutes. Use a toothpick to test for doneness.
- Remove from the oven and turn the cake upside down on a wire rack to cool.

Guglhupf (or gugelhopf) forms are available in kitchen stores and on the internet. You can also use a Bundt cake pan.

Sprinkle with powdered sugar before serving.

This recipe also works well with Lindt Excellence Madagascar 70% Cocoa, or Lindt Excellence 70% Cocoa Dark Chocolate.

Yield

8–10 servings.

Maître Chocolatier

Flora Grösslich

DARK & LIGHT TRUFFLE CAKE

THIS CAKE IS AS VISUALLY STUNNING as it is delicious.

Ingredients

Cake

Make ½ recipe of Basic Chocolate Cake (see page 145). Bake in a greased and lined 10-inch springform pan.

Coffee liqueur or coffee, enough to brush on top of the cake

Dark Layers

4 bars (3.5 ounces/100 grams each) Lindt Bittersweet Chocolate, chopped

2 cups (475 milliliters) heavy cream

White Layers

2 bars (3.5 ounces/100 grams each) Lindt Swiss Classic White Chocolate, chopped

1 ¼ cups (300 milliliters) heavy cream

Method

- Let the cake cool slightly, then remove from springform pan and transfer to a rack.
- Wash and dry the springform pan and return the cooled cake into the pan.
- Brush the liqueur or coffee onto the cake.

Layer Preparation

- First dark chocolate layer: Melt half of the dark chocolate over gently simmering water or double boiler (refer to melting methods on page 40). Let cool. Whip the cream until it is thickened, but not hard. Fold in the melted chocolate. Spread the mixture over the cake base and smooth. Gently tap the cake pan on the countertop 2 or 3 times to eliminate any air bubbles. Place in refrigerator and begin with production of the second, white chocolate layer.

- White chocolate layer: Repeat the same steps as with the dark chocolate layer. Place in the refrigerator and prepare the final dark chocolate layer.
- Second dark chocolate layer: Repeat steps as with the first dark chocolate layer. Chill in the refrigerator for a minimum of 6 hours or overnight.
- Before unlocking the springform pan, run a sharp knife around the edge.

Yield

One 10-inch cake for 8–10 servings.

Maître Chocolatier

Ann Czaja

Garnish with piped whipped cream rosettes, Lindt Thins or fresh strawberries.

This cake looks great with white and dark chocolate shavings on top.

Slice the cake with a hot knife (heated in hot water and dried), cleaning the knife between each slice.

CHOCOLATE ZUCCHINI CAKE

IT MAY SOUND ODD, but zucchini and chocolate really do complement each other in this delicious cake.

Ingredients

⅔ cup (150 grams) butter

1 cup (200 grams) sugar

3 eggs

2 tablespoons milk

1 teaspoon vanilla extract

One bar (3.5 ounces/100 grams) Lindt Bittersweet Dark Chocolate

1 ½ cups (200 grams) zucchini, finely grated

½ cup (60 grams) ground almonds

1 ⅔ cups (200 grams) flour

1 tablespoon plus 1 teaspoon baking powder

Dust with cocoa powder or powdered sugar.

This cake is a really nice addition to an end-of-the-summer party for it is a lovely celebration of the summer harvest.

Method

- Preheat oven to 350°F (180°C). Grease and line with parchment a 9-inch (23-centimeter) springform pan and set aside.
- Melt the chocolate and cool slightly.
- Sift the flour and baking powder, and set aside.
- Whip the butter, and gradually add the sugar.
- Add eggs, milk, and vanilla.
- Add the melted chocolate.
- Add the sifted ingredients and almonds.
- Stir in the zucchini.
- Bake approximately 40–50 minutes. Cake is done when a toothpick inserted in the center comes out clean.

Yield

One 9-inch cake for 8–10 servings.

Maître Chocolatier

Ann Czaja

Tarts, Cheesecakes, and Small Desserts

ZÜRICHER CHOCOLATE TART

A SWEET, BUTTERY-CHOCOLATE crust cradles the rich Lindt chocolate cream filling in this culinary tribute to Switzerland's largest city.

Ingredients

Base Chocolate Short Paste (Sweet Dough)

9 tablespoons (135 grams) butter

⅔ cup (70 grams) powdered sugar

1 egg yolk

¼ teaspoon vanilla extract

1⅔ cup (200 grams) flour

2 tablespoons cocoa powder

1–2 tablespoons cold water or milk

Filling

3 bars (3.5 ounces/100 grams each) Lindt Bittersweet Dark Chocolate, chopped

3 eggs, lightly beaten

4 egg yolks

¼ cup (50 grams) sugar

¾ cup plus 2 tablespoons (200 grams) butter

To bake blind, line the inside of the pastry with parchment paper and fill the form with uncooked rice or beans. (You can also purchase ceramic or metal weights at fine kitchen stores.) This will prevent the sides from collapsing and give the tart its shape. It will also prevent undercooked pastry on the bottom of the finished tart.

Method for the Base

- Preheat oven to 350°F (180°C).
- In a mixer or food processor, mix the butter and powdered sugar until creamed. Add the egg yolk and vanilla extract. Combine the flour and cocoa powder in a separate bowl and add to the butter mixture. If necessary, add enough of the cold water or milk to bind the dough.
- Allow dough to rest in the refrigerator for a minimum of 1 hour.
- Roll out the dough ⅛ inch (3 millimeters) thick and place in greased pan (only ½ way up springform). If using a tart form, let the dough fall over the edges of the form and roll over it with a rolling pin to crimp the dough to the tart form. Prick the bottom of the dough with a fork and bake blind.
- Bake for 10–15 minutes.

- Remove the weights. They can be reused for baking, but the beans and rice can no longer be eaten.
- Continue baking an additional 10 minutes.
- Remove the pastry from the oven, set aside and begin preparing the filling.

Method for the Filling

- Melt the chopped chocolate (see melting techniques on page 40), remove from heat and set aside.
- In a separate bowl, whip the eggs, egg yolks, and sugar until doubled in volume.
- Melt the butter.
- Add the chocolate to the egg mixture, and fold in carefully.
- Add the melted butter, gradually pouring it down the side of the mixing bowl.
- Pour the filling into the pre-baked pastry, and even out surface with a metal spatula or back of a spoon. Bake at 350°F (180°C) for 35–40 minutes.
- Cool the tart in the form. Best served at room temperature.

Yield

One 8-inch (20-centimeter) springform or tart pan with removable bottom, for 6–8 servings.

Maître Chocolatier

Ann Czaja

To finish off the tart, dust with either cocoa powder or powdered sugar. You can also use strained and heated apricot or orange preserves and paint them on the surface with a pastry brush or spread a thin coat with a spatula. To finish, sprinkle the edges with powdered sugar.

Serve the tart with a dollop of whipped cream and fresh raspberries or strawberries.

WHITE CHOCOLATE TART WITH MACADAMIA NUTS

If you use mini tart forms as shown here (between 8 and 10, depending on the size), bake for 15–20 minutes. This will give each guest their own individual tartlet.

Substitute pistachios for the macadamia nuts.

THE MACADAMIA NUTS PUNCTUATE the smooth, chocolate cream with a buttery crunch.

Ingredients

2 bars (3.5 ounces/100 grams each) Lindt Swiss Classic White Chocolate, chopped

7 tablespoons (100 grams) butter

⅔ cup (130 grams) sugar

½ teaspoon vanilla extract

2 eggs, lightly beaten

Pinch of salt

1 cup (120 grams) flour, sifted

¾ cup (110 grams) unsalted macadamia nuts, chopped

Method

- Preheat oven to 350°F (180°C). Grease and line with parchment a 9-inch (23-centimeter) springform or a 9-inch (23 centimeter) tart pan.
- Melt the chopped chocolate and butter over simmering water, in a double boiler or microwave oven. Remove from heat.
- Stir in sugar, vanilla, eggs and salt.
- Stir in flour until just combined.
- Stir in nuts.
- Pour into prepared pan. Bake approximately 20 minutes or until the tart is lightly browned. Resist the temptation to overbake.
- Cool slightly before removing from pan.
- Dust with powdered sugar.

Yield

8–10 servings.

Maître Chocolatier

Ann Czaja

SPICED MADAGASCAR TART

THIS RECIPE USES CHOCOLATE and spices from Madagascar to create an extraordinary flourless tart.

Ingredients

2 bars (3.5 ounces/100 grams each) Lindt Excellence Madagascar 70% Cocoa Chocolate, chopped

¾ cup (170 grams) butter

¼ teaspoon cinnamon, ground

¼ teaspoon coriander, ground

4 eggs, separated

1 cup (200 grams) sugar

Prior to serving, dust with cocoa powder or powdered sugar. This tart pairs well with berry coulis, fresh berries, and/or whipped cream.

To make coulis, blend and strain fresh or frozen berries and pass through a sieve. Sweeten to taste with powdered sugar.

Method

- Preheat oven to 350°F (180°C).
- Grease and line an 8- or 9-inch (20- or 23-centimeter) springform pan or tart pan with removable bottom.
- Melt the chocolate and butter (see melting techniques on page 40).
- Stir in the spices.
- In a separate bowl, combine the egg yolks with ½ cup of sugar, and whip.
- Fold the chocolate mixture into the yolks.
- Beat the egg whites, gradually adding remaining ½ cup of sugar. Beat until egg whites form stiff peaks.
- Carefully fold the egg whites into the chocolate mixture.
- Bake between 35–40 minutes. Test with a toothpick (or thin knife). If the toothpick comes out clean, the tart is finished. Do not overbake.
- This tart will sink as it cools. Cool slightly before removing from pan.

Yield

8–10 servings.

Maître Chocolatier

Ann Czaja

MOLTEN MINT CHOCOLATE CAKES

INTENSE SINGLE-SERVING cakes with a luscious, soft center.

Ingredients

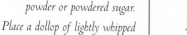

5 ounces (140 grams) Lindt Excellence Intense Mint Dark Chocolate, chopped

¾ cup plus 2 tablespoons (200 grams) butter

3 eggs

3 egg yolks

1 ½ cup (150 grams) powdered sugar

1 teaspoon vanilla extract

¼ teaspoon mint extract

½ cup (60 grams) flour

To garnish, dust with cocoa powder or powdered sugar. Place a dollop of lightly whipped cream on the side and top with a sprig of fresh mint.

Method

- Preheat oven to 450°F (230°C).
- Brush the inside of each ramekin with melted butter and coat the inside of each with sugar, knocking out any excess.
- Melt the chocolate and butter (see melting techniques on page 40).
- Whip eggs, egg yolks, sugar, vanilla and mint extracts on high power for 10 minutes.
- Fold the melted chocolate and butter into the egg mixture.
- Fold in the flour until just combined.
- Divide the batter among the ramekins.
- Bake for 8–10 minutes. The sides and top should be set, but the center will remain soft. Do not overbake.
- Let the cakes rest for 3–5 minutes before unmolding.
- To loosen, run a small, sharp knife around the edge of the ramekin and carefully turn out onto a plate.

Yield

Six 4-ounce (120-milliliter) ramekins.

Maître Chocolatier

Ann Czaja

MILK CHOCOLATE ALMOND CHEESECAKE

Top this cake with milk chocolate shavings and dust with cocoa powder.

MILK CHOCOLATE AND ALMOND pair beautifully to make this cheesecake something special.

Ingredients

Base

2 cups (175 grams) vanilla wafers, ground

½ cup (60 grams) almonds, ground

3 tablespoons (45 grams) butter, melted

Filling

3 bars (3.5 ounces/100 grams each) Lindt Swiss Classic Milk Chocolate, chopped

24 ounces (672 grams) cream cheese, softened

½ cup (100 grams) sugar

¾ cup (180 milliliters) sour cream

4 eggs

1 teaspoon almond extract

Optional

One bar (3.5 ounces/100 grams) Lindt Swiss Classic Milk Chocolate to decorate

Method for the Base

- Preheat oven to 350°F (180°C).
- Place vanilla wafers in a food processor and blend until finely ground.
- Add almonds and melted butter.
- Press into the bottom of a greased 9-inch (23-centimeter) springform pan.

Method for the Filling

- Melt chopped chocolate (see melting techniques on page 40) and set aside.
- Combine cream cheese, sugar, and sour cream and beat until smooth. Scrape down the sides of the bowl to avoid lumps.
- Add eggs and almond extract.
- Stir in melted chocolate.
- Pour the batter into prepared springform pan. Bake for 15 minutes at 350°F (180°C).
- Decrease oven temperature to 200°F (93°C) and bake for 1 hour and 10 minutes or until the center of the cake is set. Remove the cake from oven and run a knife around the edge of the springform. This will help to prevent cracking.
- Turn off the oven and return the cake to the oven for an additional hour.
- Chill overnight.
- To serve, cut with a wet knife dipped in hot water.

Yield

One 9-inch (23-centimeter) springform pan for 8–10 servings.

Maître Chocolatier

Ann Czaja

CHOCOLATE ORANGE CHEESECAKE

THIS CHEESECAKE IS BAKED in a water bath to ensure extra creaminess.

Ingredients

Base

    1 ⅓ cups (250 grams) vanilla wafers, ground

    ⅔ cup (150 grams) butter, melted

Filling

    20 ounces (575 grams) cream cheese

    ¼ cup (60 grams) sour cream

    ⅔ cup (130 grams) sugar

    ⅓ cup plus 1 tablespoon (100 milliliters) orange juice

    2 bars (3.5 ounces/100 grams each) Lindt Excellence Intense Orange Chocolate, chopped

    4 eggs

Method for the Base

- Preheat oven to 250°F (120°C).
- Grease a 10-inch (25-centimeter) springform pan.
- Place the vanilla wafers in a food processor and blend till finely ground. Add enough melted butter until the mixture just binds together.
- Press the mixture evenly into the base of the springform pan and smooth it with the back of a spoon.
- Encase the bottom half of the pan in aluminum foil. The cheesecake will be baked in a water bath and this step ensures that no water will seep in.

Method for the Filling

- Beat the cream cheese until smooth, scraping down the sides of bowl to prevent lumps.
- Add the sour cream and sugar. Continue mixing until smooth.
- Place the orange juice in a saucepan and gently bring to the boil.

This cake is best made a day in advance, allowing it sufficient time to cool and settle. This recipe is very versatile and the Excellence Intense Orange can easily be substituted with other Lindt chocolate.

Try a milk chocolate espresso cheesecake. Just substitute strong coffee for the orange juice and Excellence Extra Creamy Milk Chocolate for the Intense Orange.

- Add the chopped chocolate, remove from the heat, and stir until completely melted.
- Mix the orange/chocolate mixture into the cheese mixture, scraping down the sides of the bowl.
- Add the eggs one at a time, mixing well after each addition.
- Transfer the cheesecake mixture to the prepared springform pan and put into a baking pan deep enough to hold an inch of water.
- Put cheesecake into oven and pour an inch of very hot water into the baking pan.
- Bake for approximately 45 minutes. The cake is ready when it is set on the sides, but remains slightly soft in the center.
- Cool in the springform pan.

Yield

One 10-inch (25-centimeter) springform pan for 8–10 servings.

Maître Chocolatier

Thomas Schnetzler

ORANGE CRÊPE SOUFFLÉ WITH CHOCOLATE SAUCE

THIS RECIPE COMBINES THE simplicity of a crêpe with the complexity of a soufflé. Top it off with chocolate sauce and the combination is complete.

Ingredients

Crêpes

1 cup plus 2 tablespoons (250 grams) flour

Pinch of salt

¼ cup (40 grams) sugar

3 eggs

2 cups (475 milliliters) milk

3 tablespoons (40 grams) butter, melted

3 teaspoons orange liqueur

Oil or melted butter for cooking

Orange Soufflé "Basic"

2 cups (475 milliliters) milk

3 tablespoons of candied orange or fresh orange peel (approximately 2–3 inches long)

4 egg yolks

⅔ cup (125 grams) sugar

½ cup (50 grams) flour

Before serving

4 tablespoons orange liqueur

2 egg yolks

8 egg whites

⅓ cup (60 grams) sugar

As with a traditional soufflé, this dessert should be plated and served as soon as it comes out of the oven. Have the dessert plates and chocolate ready to go.

Decorate with chocolate sauce, orange peel, or mint leaves.

Serve the finished crêpe on a plate with the chocolate sauce and desired garnish or whipped cream.

Method for the crêpe

■ Mix the flour, salt, and sugar in a bowl. Make a well in the middle of the dry ingredients.

- Add the eggs, and then slowly add the milk. Whisk constantly. The mix has to be perfectly smooth.
- Let rest in the fridge for 30 minutes.
- Add the melted butter and orange liqueur to the mix. Whisk until smooth.
- To cook the crêpes, use a short-sided skillet with open rather than curved sides.
  - On medium heat, melt about 1 tablespoon of unsalted butter in the pan.
  - Before pouring the first crêpe, flick a drop of water on the pan; if it sizzles, the pan is ready. A hot pan is key but you don't want to burn the butter; getting the temperature just right is the main challenge.
  - Have your bowl of batter, a ladle, and an empty bowl or cup ready by the stove.
  - Ladle about two tablespoons of the batter into the hot pan, and swiftly coat the entire bottom by tilting and gently swirling the batter all around the pan, allowing any excess to run off into the other bowl or cup.
  - Cook for about two minutes or until the top is glossy and the edges curl slightly. Turn gently with a spatula or fork, and cook two more minutes.
  - Place on a piece of wax or parchment paper. Put a small pat of butter into the pan and stir the batter between each crêpe.
- Cover the crêpes and reserve.

Method for the Soufflé

- Heat the milk with the candied orange or orange peel in a saucepan.
- In a separate saucepan, mix the 4 egg yolks and sugar until combined. Add the flour and mix well.
- If using fresh orange peel, remove it from the milk.
- Pour the hot milk into the yolk mixture. Heat it until it is thickened and just starts to bubble.
- Pour the mixture into a bowl and set aside. This is the soufflé "basic."

Just before Serving

- Add the orange liqueur and 2 egg yolks to the basic.
- Beat the egg whites, gradually adding the sugar, until they form stiff peaks.
- Fold the egg white mixture into the basic.

CHOCOLATE SAUCE

Ingredients

⅓ cup (80 milliliters) heavy cream

1 cup (240 milliliters) milk

3 tablespoons sugar

Pinch of salt

2 bars (3.5 ounces/100 grams each) Lindt Excellence
   70% Cocoa Dark Chocolate, chopped

1 ½ tablespoons (20 grams) butter

Method

- Heat the cream with the milk, sugar, and salt.
- Add the chopped chocolate.
- Let boil briefly while stirring.
- Pour into a bowl and add the butter.

Assembly

- Fill each crêpe with 3 tablespoons of soufflé.
- Fold the crêpe in half, forming a half circle.
- Lay the crêpes on a baking sheet lined with parchment paper and dust with powdered sugar.
- Bake for 10 minutes at 400°F (200°C). The crêpe should double in volume.
- See page 185 for serving tips.

Yield

8 servings.

Maîtres Chocolatiers

Hélène Mazuyer, Jean-Pierre Larramendy, & David Vignau

CHOUX WITH CHOCOLATE CREAM FILLING

To serve as a plated dessert, make the chocolate sauce from the Classic Panna Cotta recipe on page 93. Pour some of the sauce on a plate and swirl it around or spread with the back of a spoon. This is referred to as a "mirror."

Place 3 of the filled choux buns on the plate and dust with powdered sugar or cocoa powder.

POPULARLY KNOWN AS CREAM PUFFS, these little treats can be served from a tray or plated as a dessert.

Ingredients

Pâte à Choux (pronounced "Shoe")
¾ cup (180 milliliters) milk
½ cup (120 milliliters) water
2 tablespoons (25 grams) sugar
½ teaspoon salt
⅔ cups (150 grams) butter
2 cups (240 grams) flour
6 eggs, slightly beaten

Method

- Preheat oven to 400°F (200°C).
- Combine the milk, water, sugar, salt, and butter in a saucepan and bring to a boil.
- Add the flour and stir until the liquid is absorbed. Continue stirring the flour mixture over moderate heat for 5 minutes.
- Transfer the flour mixture into a mixing bowl and beat on low speed to cool. Mixture should be lukewarm when the eggs are added.
- Start to add the eggs. The final dough should be shiny and smooth. You may need more egg to achieve this.
- Using a pastry bag and star tip (size #15 will work fine), pipe small rosettes onto baking trays lined with parchment paper.
- Bake 10 minutes, then decrease oven temperature to 375°F (190°C) and bake an additional 10 minutes, or until golden brown. Do not open oven door while baking.
- Transfer to a wire rack and let cool completely.

CHOCOLATE CREAM FILLING

Ingredients

    1 cup (240 milliliters) heavy cream
    ½ bar (3.5 ounces/100 grams each) Lindt Swiss Classic Milk or Bittersweet
       Chocolate, chopped

Method

- Heat the cream in a saucepan over medium heat; remove from heat and stir in the chopped chocolate.
- Stir until the chocolate is completely melted.
- Transfer to a bowl and refrigerate 6 hours or overnight.
- Before using, whip the chilled cream with a mixer until it is light and airy.

Assembly

- Cut the choux in half.
- Place the whipped chocolate cream in a pastry bag with a star tip.
- Pipe cream into the bottom halves of the choux. Alternatively the cream can be placed onto the choux with a teaspoon.
- Replace tops and press down lightly.
- Dust with powdered sugar or cocoa powder, place on tray and serve.

Yield

Makes between 30 and 40 choux. To serve this as a dessert you will need 3 per person. The remainder can be frozen.

Maître Chocolatier

Ann Czaja

CHOCOLATE STRUDEL WITH CHERRY COMPOTE

STRUDEL IS TRADITIONALLY MADE with a special dough and filled with apples. This version uses phyllo dough, cherries and chocolate.

Ingredients

6 to 8 large sheets of phyllo dough

Filling

2.5 ounces (75 grams) Lindt Bittersweet Dark or Swiss Classic Milk Chocolate (half of each works well too), chopped

⅓ cup (75 grams) butter, softened

1 ounce (28 grams) marzipan

4 eggs, separated

½ teaspoon vanilla extract

Pinch of salt

¼ cup (50 grams) sugar

1 cup (120 grams) almonds, ground

¼ cup (60 grams) butter for assembly of strudel

To serve, cut the strudel and place a piece on a plate. Spoon some of the cherry compote on the side and dust with powdered sugar. You can also serve with whipped cream or a scoop of vanilla ice cream.

Method

- Melt the chopped chocolate (see melting techniques on page 40). Set aside.
- Whip butter and add marzipan, egg yolks, vanilla extract and salt.
- Add the melted chocolate.
- Whip egg whites, gradually adding sugar, and beat to stiff peaks.
- Fold the egg whites into the chocolate mixture.
- Fold in the ground almonds.

Assembly

- Lay down a phyllo sheet on a clean, large kitchen towel or small tablecloth. Sprinkle with melted butter. Place a second sheet about half way down the first and sprinkle with butter. Repeat this alternating pattern until you have one large piece of dough.

- Place the filling toward the front of the dough, forming a thick log from end to end.
- Pick up the end of the cloth nearest to you and begin to roll the dough over the filling. Make sure the dough is actually rolling under before proceeding.
- Finish pulling the cloth away from you, which will roll the strudel.
- Carefully transfer strudel to a baking tray lined with parchment paper. Tuck ends underneath and brush with butter. Take a few more phyllo sheets and wrap them around the strudel, buttering between the layers and on the surface.
- It is important that the seams of the dough are tucked underneath the strudel or it will open during baking and the filling will seep out. Adding a few extra sheets of dough will strengthen the strudel.
- Bake at 350°F (180°C) for 25–30 minutes, or until golden brown. Cool slightly before serving. See serving suggestions on page 191.

CHERRY COMPOTE

Ingredients

2 cups (375 grams) frozen cherries

1 tablespoon sugar

1 tablespoon rum (optional)

1 teaspoon cornstarch

- Place the cherries, sugar, and rum in a saucepan and cook over medium heat.
- Mix the cornstarch with enough cold water to form a paste.
- Add cornstarch paste to the cherries and cook for 1 to 2 minutes.
- Remove the thickened cherries from the heat.

Yield

5–6 servings.

Maître Chocolatier

Hans Geller

CHOCOLATE SOUFFLÉ

THIS IS A CLASSIC DESSERT that has a reputation for being very fussy. The secret to successful soufflés is to follow the directions step by step and never open the oven door while the soufflés are baking. Serve immediately before the soufflés begin to deflate.

Ingredients

¼ cup (55 grams) butter

⅓ cup plus 2 tablespoons (55 grams) flour

½ cup (125 milliliters) milk

1.4 ounces (40 grams) Lindt Excellence 70% Cocoa Dark Chocolate, chopped

⅓ cup (40 grams) cocoa powder

5 egg whites

4 egg yolks

⅓ cup (65 grams) sugar

Melted butter and sugar to prepare soufflé forms

The basic soufflé recipe without the egg whites can be made in advance and stored in the refrigerator. Before baking, remove from fridge, warm slightly over water bath, whip egg whites and sugar and proceed as directed.

Try substituting other Lindt dark chocolate including Madagascar, Intense Mint, or Bittersweet.

Method

- Preheat oven to 400°F (200°C).
- Prepare forms/form by coating the inside with melted butter and sprinkling with sugar. Tap out any excess sugar.
- Put the butter and flour in a bowl and knead together. Roll into a rope and cut into small pieces.
- Put the milk, chopped chocolate, and cocoa powder in a saucepan and bring to a boil over medium heat, stirring continuously.
- Add the flour/butter pieces and stir until smooth and thickened.
- Remove the saucepan from the heat and stir in one egg white.
- Pour the mixture into a bowl and cool until lukewarm.
- Add the egg yolks one at a time, stirring.
- Whip the remaining egg whites, gradually adding the sugar until they form stiff peaks.
- Carefully fold the whipped egg whites into the chocolate mixture.
- Spoon the soufflé mixture into the prepared forms.

- Place the forms in a large baking pan. Fill the baking pan with very hot water up to the middle of the forms, and place in lower third of the oven.
- Reduce the oven temperature to 375°F (190°C).
- Bake for 25–30 minutes for small forms or 35–40 minutes for large form.
- Never open the oven door when making a soufflé!
- Prepare serving plates and powdered sugar while the soufflés are baking.
- When finished, remove from the oven, set the souffé in its form on dessert plate, sprinkle with powdered sugar, and serve. A soufflé will hold its shape for a few minutes.

Yield

Eight 4-ounce (120-milliliter) ramekins, or one 7-inch (18-centimeter) large soufflé form, for 8 servings.

Maître Chocolatier

Hans Geller

CHOCOLATE GANACHE TART

THIS TART IS SMOOTH, rich, and decadent.

Ingredients

Short Paste (Sweet Dough)

½ cup plus 1 tablespoon (130 grams) butter

⅔ cup (70 grams) powdered sugar

1 egg yolk

¼ teaspoon vanilla extract

1⅔ cup (200 grams) flour

1–2 tablespoons of cold water or milk

1 egg yolk to brush on pastry

Filling

3¾ cups (875 milliliters) heavy cream

⅓ cup (65 grams) sugar

12½ oz (375 grams) Lindt Excellence 70% Cocoa Dark Chocolate, chopped

1 egg

4 egg yolks

Pinch of salt

To bake blind, line the inside of the pastry with parchment paper and fill the form with uncooked rice or beans. (You can also purchase ceramic or metal weights at fine kitchen stores.) This will prevent the sides from collapsing and give the tart its shape. It will also prevent undercooked pastry on the bottom of the finished tart.

Method for the Dough

- In a mixer or food processor, mix butter and sugar until creamed. Add egg yolk and vanilla extract. Add flour to butter mixture. Add just enough liquid until the dough binds.
- Allow to rest in refrigerator a minimum of 1 hour.
- Roll out dough ⅛ inch (3-millimeter) thick and place in greased pan (only halfway up springform). If using a tart form let it fall over the edges of the form and roll over it with a rolling pin. Prick the bottom of the dough with a fork and bake blind (see sidebar).

- Bake at 350°F (180°C) for 10–15 minutes.
- Remove the rice/beans or weights. The rice/beans can be reused for baking, but can no longer be eaten.
- Continue baking an additional 10 minutes. Brush with egg yolk and return to oven briefly just to glaze the egg.
- Remove from the oven, set aside, and let cool while you begin the filling.

Method for the Filling

- Mix together the cream and sugar in a saucepan and bring to a boil over medium heat.
- Remove from heat and add the chocolate. Stir until the chocolate has completely melted and the mixture is smooth.
- Put the egg and egg yolks into a separate bowl and whisk. Pour the chocolate mixture into the eggs and add pinch of salt. Mix well.
- Gently pour the tart mixture into the prepared crust and bake approximately 45 minutes or until just set in the center.
- While the tart is still hot, use a sharp knife to cut off excess pastry at the rim of the chocolate filling, giving the tart a straight edge. Let the mixture cool in the springform.
- Serve at room temperature.

Yield

Two 9-inch (23-centimeter) 1-inch-deep fluted tart pans, or one 9- or 10-inch (23- or 24-centimeter) springform pan for 10–12 servings.

Maître Chocolatier

Thomas Schnetzler

Bake the tart a day in advance or early the same day as needed. This will give the tart time to set and make it easier to cut.

Serve with whipped cream and fresh berries.

Chocolate Drinks

CLASSIC HOT CHOCOLATE

THE MOVIE *CHOCOLAT* inspired the Maîtres Chocolatiers of Lindt to create this superb hot chocolate.

Ingredients

1 quart (1 liter) milk

1 Madagascar vanilla bean, split

1 stick of cinnamon

¾ teaspoon (3.5 grams) black peppercorns (whole)

2 bars (3.5 ounces/100 grams each) Lindt Excellence Madagascar 70% Cocoa, chopped

Method

- Heat the milk with the spices in a saucepan over medium heat until it reaches boiling point, but do not let the milk boil.
- Add the chopped chocolate and whisk until smooth.
- Remove from heat and let rest for 25 minutes to release the spices' aroma.
- Strain the liquid and reheat before serving.

Yield

4–6 servings.

Maîtres Chocolatiers

Jean-Pierre Larramendy, Hélène Mazuyer, & David Vignau

Serve hot with a tablespoon of whipped cream. Sprinkle with chocolate shavings.

Try using Excellence 70% Cocoa or Ecuador 75% Cocoa for a darker drink.

Remove the black pepper for a less spicy drink.

SPICY HOT CHOCOLATE

THIS BEVERAGE PAYS HOMAGE to cocoa's origins, when long ago the Maya and Aztec revered it and combined it with another bountiful fruit, the chili, into a spicy and invigorating drink.

Ingredients

1 cup (240 milliliters) whole milk

1 cup (240 milliliters) heavy cream

1 vanilla bean, split

1 cinnamon stick

1 red chili pepper, split and deseeded

½ bar (3.5 ounces/100 grams each) Lindt Excellence 70% Cocoa, chopped

Optional

Lightly whipped cream and ground cinnamon to garnish

Method

- Combine milk and cream with vanilla bean, cinnamon stick, and chili pepper. Heat to a heavy simmer.
- Add chocolate and whisk until completely dissolved. Remove from heat and let it rest for 15 minutes.
- Strain the liquid and return it to the saucepan. Scrape any remaining seeds from the vanilla bean and whisk back into the hot chocolate.
- Reheat before serving.

Yield

2–3 servings.

Maître Chocolatier

Ann Czaja

The Aztec served their chocolate drink frothy by pouring it between two vessels. This effect can be recreated by whisking the hot chocolate until it is frothy.

For a more modern version, serve with a dollop of lightly whipped cream and dust with ground cinnamon.

For a lighter drink, replace the cream with half & half or with milk.

HOT WHITE CHOCOLATE

SMALL CAPS Enjoy this creamy hot drink made with white chocolate and a touch of Irish cream. For a lighter drink replace the heavy cream with half & half or milk.

The alcohol isn't necessary to enjoy this rich drink. You can omit it and flavor the hot chocolate with vanilla. Use half of a vanilla pod; scrape the seeds and add both seeds and pod to the milk and cream. Remove the pod before serving. You can also use vanilla extract, but use only about ¼ teaspoon.

Ingredients

1 cup (240 milliliters) whole milk

1 cup (240 milliliters) heavy cream

½ bar (3.5 ounces/100 grams each) Lindt Swiss Classic White Chocolate, chopped

¼ cup (60 milliliters) Irish cream liqueur

Optional

Lightly whipped cream to garnish

Cocoa powder

Method

- In a saucepan, heat the milk and cream to a simmer.
- Reduce heat and add the chopped chocolate, stirring until completely dissolved.
- Remove from the heat and stir in the liqueur.
- Pour the hot beverage into a mug. If desired, garnish with whipped cream, and dust with cocoa powder.

Yield

2–3 servings.

Maître Chocolatier

Ann Czaja

GRASSHOPPER HOT CHOCOLATE

HOT CHOCOLATE WITH A TOUCH of mint. Enjoy it by the fireplace!

For a lighter drink, replace the cream with half & half or milk.

Ingredients

1 cup (240 milliliters) whole milk

1 cup (240 milliliters) heavy cream

½ bar (3.5 ounces/100 grams each) Lindt Excellence Intense Mint, chopped

¼ cup (60 milliliters) crème de menthe

2 tablespoons (30 milliliters) crème de cacao

Optional

Lightly whipped cream and Lindt Intense Mint shavings to garnish

Method

- Combine the milk and cream in a saucepan and bring to a heavy simmer.
- Add in the chopped chocolate and stir until completely melted.
- Remove from the heat and stir in the liqueurs.
- Serve in warmed mugs. Garnish with whipped cream and chocolate shavings if desired.

Yield

2–3 servings.

Maître Chocolatier

Ann Czaja

BASIC CHOCOLATE MILK

THIS RECIPE IS SIMPLE and delicious. We are never too old to enjoy a glass of chocolate milk.

Ingredients

To make simple syrup

2 tablespoons water

2 tablespoons (25 grams) sugar

1 ⅓ cups (400 milliliters) milk

2 tablespoons simple syrup

2.5 ounces (70 grams) Lindt Bittersweet Chocolate, chopped

Method

- Combine the water and sugar in a saucepan and bring to a boil. When the sugar is dissolved, remove the saucepan from the heat. Set aside.
- Heat the milk and syrup to 122–140°F (50–60°C) and add the chopped chocolate.
- Whisk until the chocolate is melted.
- Refrigerate until chilled.

Yield

2–3 servings.

Maître Chocolatier

Urs Liechti

This chocolate milk is terrific as is, or can be used in the recipes for Costa Rica Drink and Jamaica Drink.

ICED MOCHA

A RICH AND DELICIOUS version of iced coffee.

Ingredients

2 ½ cups (600 milliliters) milk

1 bar (3.5 ounces/100 grams each) Lindt Excellence 70% Cocoa Dark Chocolate, chopped

1 cup (240 milliliters) strong coffee

⅛ teaspoon ground cinnamon

¼ cup (60 milliliters) crème de cacao or other chocolate liqueur (optional)

Garnish with a sprig of fresh mint and a cinnamon stick.

Method

- In a small saucepan, heat 1 cup of the milk.
- Add the chopped chocolate, stirring until completely melted.
- Stir in the coffee and cinnamon; remove from heat.
- Cool to room temperature.
- Add remaining milk and crème de cacao, and chill until ready to serve.

To Serve

Shake and strain into a tall glass with ice, or, for a more elegant presentation, use a martini glass.

Yield

4–5 servings.

Maître Chocolatier

Hans Mazenauer

WHITE CHOCOLATE STRAWBERRY DRINK

IT IS NO SECRET THAT STRAWBERRIES and chocolate are fantastic together. Try them in this refreshing drink.

Ingredients

2 cups (475 milliliters) milk

1 bar (3.5 ounces/100 grams each) Lindt Swiss Classic White Chocolate, chopped

5 fresh strawberries

¼ cup white rum (optional)

Method

- Heat the milk in a saucepan, and add the chopped chocolate. Remove the saucepan from heat and stir until completely melted.
- Refrigerate until completely cooled.

To Serve

Clean and chop the strawberries. Combine the white chocolate milk mixture with the berries in a blender. Blend until combined. Strain and stir in the rum. Serve in chilled glasses.

Yield

2–3 servings.

Maître Chocolatier

Ann Czaja

Try substituting raspberries for the strawberries. You'll need to add the same approximate weight or measure as the 5 strawberries.

PINEAPPLE COCONUT COCKTAIL

A CHOCOLATE INSPIRED version of a piña colada.

Ingredients

2 ½ cups (600 milliliters) pineapple juice

1 bar (3.5 ounces/100 grams) Lindt White Excellence Coconut, chopped

¼ cup (60 milliliters) rum

⅓ cup (80 milliliters) coconut liqueur

⅔ cup (160 milliliters) crushed ice

Method

■ Heat the pineapple juice in a saucepan until it comes to a boil, then remove from heat.

■ Stir in the chocolate. Continue stirring until completely melted.

■ Add the rum and coconut liqueur.

■ Chill completely. Shake or whisk before serving.

■ Serve in tall glasses over crushed ice.

You can also serve this drink in martini glasses with a garnish of sliced pineapple.

Yield

4–5 servings.

Maître Chocolatier

Hans Mazenauer

COSTA RICA DRINK

*Garnish with grated
Excellence Madagascar
70% Cocoa.*

THE RUM IN THIS DRINK IS OPTIONAL, but complements the chocolate
and banana beautifully.

Ingredients

>   1 recipe of Basic Chocolate Milk (page 211) using Lindt Swiss Bittersweet Chocolate
>   1 medium ripe banana (100 grams), peeled and sliced
>   2 tablespoons white rum (optional)

Method

- Prepare Basic Chocolate Milk as directed and chill.
- Prior to serving, blend the chocolate milk and banana in a blender until smooth. Add the rum if desired.
- Serve in chilled glasses.

Yield

2–3 servings.

Maître Chocolatier

Urs Liechti

JAMAICA DRINK

THIS IS A VERSION OF CHOCOLATE MILK that is specifically for adults. The rum and the 70% make a very beautiful pairing.

Ingredients

> 1 Recipe of Basic Chocolate Milk (see page 211) using Lindt Excellence 70% Cocoa Dark Chocolate
>
> 2 tablespoons brown rum

Method

- Prepare Basic Chocolate Milk as directed and let cool.
- Prior to serving add 2 tablespoons of rum and stir.
- Serve in chilled glasses or over ice.

Yield

2–3 servings.

Maître Chocolatier

Urs Liechti

If you'd rather visit Ecuador than Jamaica, use Lindt Excellence Ecuador 75% Cocoa in the Basic Chocolate Milk recipe and substitute coffee liqueur for the rum.

CHOCOLATE RASPBERRY "LINDTINI"

THIS ELEGANTLY DECADENT martini uses the magic of crème de cacao and replaces the traditional olive garnish with a luscious Lindor truffle.

Ingredients

3 ounces (90 milliliters) raspberry vodka

2 ounces (60 milliliters) white crème de cacao

Garnish

Lindor Raspberry or 60% Dark truffles

Fresh raspberries

Method

- Chill the vodka and crème de cacao.
- Chill 2 martini glasses.
- Put the vodka and crème de cacao into a cocktail shaker filled with ice. Shake and pour into the chilled martini glasses.
- Add truffle and a fresh raspberry.

Yield

2 servings.

Maître Chocolatier

Ann Czaja

INDEX

SPECIAL THANKS to those who collaborated on our recipes: Kelly Malone, for the White Chocolate Bark with Peppermint & Dark Chocolate Drizzle, page 62; Brian Flanagan, for the German Chocolate Cake, page 149; and Edward Kraus, for the Chocolate Raspberry "Lindtini," page 223.

Photography on the following pages used by permission: page 4, Late classic Maya vase, © Justin Kerr, K6418; Aztec sculpture on page 4 from the collection of the National Anthropology and History Museum of Mexico, reprinted under the terms of the GNU Free Documentation License, Version 1.2; photo on page 5, © Punchstock; page 28, photo of ripening cacao pods by Medicaster.

Lindt Photography: pages viii, 3, 7–10, 12, 13, 15–17, 18, 20–26, 31, 32, 34, 38, 51, 54–55, 57, 61, 68, 69, 82, 101, 129 (bottom), 134, 157, 167, 176, 181 (top), 185, 190–191, 199, 203, 206, 224.

Jim Scherer Photography: cover, and pages ii, 14, 18 (Ann Czaja), 36, 37, 40–48, 52, 56, 58–60, 62–67, 70–81, 83–100, 102–129, 130–133, 135–156, 158–165, 168–172, 174–175, 177–183, 187–189, 192–198, 200–202, 204–205, 207–223.

CREDITS